WHAT DOES IT FEEL LIKE BEING BORN?

A memoir of maternity activism

Jodie Miller

This is a work of narrative non-fiction. The story is accurate to the author's account and records and as corroborated by colleagues. While all events are true, some identifying names and details have been changed. Some events have been compressed and people merged for reader's enjoyment. Dialogues are reflections of real conversations, without embellishment.

Printed in Australia

First Printing: Nov 2020

Shawline Publishing Group Pty Ltd
www.shawlinepublishing.com.au

Paperback ISBN- 9781922444158

Ebook ISBN- 9781922444165

For all the healers of birth.

A lifetime ago in Japan, my teacher colleagues were recounting stories over lunchboxes in the staff room. As a student of Japanese, my speaking skills were patchy, but my listening vocabulary was improving every day. My teacher-friend, Yumiko, explained how she was bathing with her three-year-old son. She'd asked him,

'Umaretatoki, nan to iu kimochi?'

Literally, 'What did it feel like when you were born?'

She'd used 'to be born' in the passive, *umareru*.

Was she asking, do you remember being a baby? Or being born? Both struck me as ludicrous. Babies aren't sentient in that way. I was certain of it.

Our small group of women listened in awe as she recounted his response, gesturing to the junction where the four frontal and parietal bones met at the top of her skull, the place where a newborn has a soft spot after birth.

'Atama itaku'te; te ga kou'te,' He said, my head hurt and my hands were like this. Then she crossed her arms tightly to her chest. The other teachers gasped and clucked.

'Sou nan desuka? Sugoi desu ne!' they said. Really? That's incredible!

The hairs prickled on the back of my neck as I visualised the position of a baby being born; cone head, arms pressed to the body in a squeeze.

My head hurt. My hands were like this.

I was still young and fearful of everything procreational. I had never conceived of the notion that a baby not only feels its own birth but has the potential to remember it three years later. Could it be a memory buried deep within all of us?

There is such a special sweetness in being able to participate in creation... Pamela Nadav

1 AN ULTIMATUM

April 1998

It's late, and we're drunk.

After three years in Tokyo, we're back on Australia's east coast to find marriages dissolved, new relationships formed, babies born and children grown, all in our irrelevant absence.

The party is over. Paul, my husband, just escorted his best mate to a taxi. That much hasn't changed. Vincent always was the last to leave. Paul's mother went to bed an hour ago. We carefully finish the dishes for her without knowing where things go.

Paul leans against the bench, running his fingers through his long curly hair. Everyone was so surprised to see it.

'You worried me tonight.' His tone takes me back to old arguments and the booze isn't likely to help.

'What do you mean?'

'Kay asked if we plan to start a family, and you scoffed. I want children. I always thought you did, too.'

'I do.'

'When?'

I can imagine being a mother someday, but it's more of a fantasy: packing school lunches, kissing Paul as he leaves for work, driving the kids to school, and taking myself to work.

Pregnancy holds no romance. Childbirth is unimaginable. Lactation repulses me. I've never experienced the urge to sniff other people's babies.

'What about our trek through South East Asia?' I pout. We'd postponed it so Paul could return to Brisbane for his dream job. He promised we'd go.

'We can do it with a baby.'

'Really, it's that easy?

'When?' he repeats, blinking. Blue eyes. I know his face so well.

'I don't know.'

'Come on. You can do better than that.'

'I can't, Paul. I just don't feel it.'

'But I do, Jodie. Can't you see?'

I see it. Clear as day. Paul was so natural tonight, interacting with his young nieces and nephews, cuddling his brother's new baby.

I was the opposite, recoiling from a toddler's slobbery touch, an awkward woman with no nurturing instinct.

'Just give me some time.'

'We've been married six years, Jodie. We'll be thirty soon. How much more time do you need?'

Silence.

'I need to know,' he flips the tea towel over his shoulder with a cold waft of Morning Fresh, 'because if you never want kids then our marriage won't work.'

My face grows hot. I know what he's saying.

'Give me a time.'

'How can I do that?' This man. He was tenacious enough to propose three times. He doesn't take no for an answer.

'By the time you're thirty. Is that unreasonable?' He returns his attention to the dishes in the drainer.

Unreasonable? Hell yes! I need to find work as a teacher. Didn't we go all the way to Japan to give me experience? I've only just registered with the Board of Education. Doesn't he realise the irreversible disruption he's inviting into our lives?

And what about me? Easy for him. There will be no hardship in impregnating me. He won't have to endure a pregnancy and birth or bear the burden of expectation to give up his career and raise a baby. Or *work* and raise a baby.

What about my body? I'm only just learning to like it in my late twenties. What about stretch marks? And...down there?

How am I supposed to decide? Once you have a baby, you can't send it back. He's giving me less than two years. I feel cheated by his ultimatum.

'So, what's your answer?' He wipes his hands on the tea towel. 'Thirty?'

I scan his mother's living room; the dusty fan whirring on its pedestal, and the wall of wedding photos, including Paul and me.

There's no way I can win this argument. He wants an answer now. I don't have one that will satisfy him. So, I lie.

'Yes.' I give the plug in the sink a yank.

'Really? Great!' He hugs me, elated.

The dishwater spirals down the drain with a loud sucking sound.

I hug him back and resign myself to divorce if I change my mind.

May 1999

South East Asia is not in our future. Our Japanese savings become a mortgage on a three-bedroom house in the suburbs, smack bang between three primary schools. We move in, get private health insurance like Prime Minister John Howard is urging everyone to do, and stop using birth control. I'm still ambivalent about motherhood, but I love my husband.

It figures that he's the first to notice. I'm catching the last rays of autumn with a good book while he generates the comforting smell of cut grass on our tiny patch of lawn. He stops by me, kills the motor, and runs his sweaty hands over his fresh crew cut.

'You look different today.' His eyes dip to my bust line and I know what he's thinking.

'Don't be silly,' I flirt. I'm wearing my favourite top and yes, I can see what he sees. 'My period might be due.'

'Due when?'

I cast my mind back to the last time I put an X on the calendar. I never was very disciplined about that. I write 'pregnancy test' on the shopping list.

Too impatient to wait, Paul makes a special trip. I try not to be annoyed by his exuberance.

My GP is in her 40s and Dutch, I think. She uses a plastic pipette to put a drop of my urine onto a circle of paper. An instant blue halo forms, confirming the result from Clearblue.

'Congratulations. That was easy, hey? Some couples take years.' Her accent makes it a matter of fact, but I also hear a tiny sorrow. She gestures to a photo frame on her bookshelf, 'My children are three and five.'

Out of a drawer, she takes a cardboard wheel attached to a second wheel via a split pin through the centre. She asks when I had my last menstrual period, the last time I had sex and other personal questions, then turns the dial and suggests a due date close to Valentine's Day.

'An ultrasound will clear up any doubt. Have you thought about your birth options?'

'Er, not really.' Meaning, not at all. I'm currently focused on not freaking out that there's a tiny parasite in my uterus.

'I suggest you go home and register for the Birth Centre at the Royal Women's Hospital.' She rifles through a box of index cards and writes a phone number on memo paper, passing it to me. 'Call today. It's extremely popular. If you wait, you might miss out.'

'I will,' I reply. Then I add, 'Thank you,' because despite not feeling especially maternal, I take pride in my manners.

By that afternoon, I've put my name on a waiting list. I know nothing about the Birth Centre. I'm just following my doctor's advice.

One week later, I wake up with blood in my underwear. Ambivalence evaporates, precipitating doubt, which pools as fear. Paul suggests we call and ask our GP to fit me in.

'I'm sorry, Jodie,' she says. 'You could come in, and it could be nothing, just a normal part of growing life and I can't help you. Or it could be something, in which case it's a normal part of growing life and I can't help you. I advise you to rest. Stay in bed today and go to the hospital if you have more bleeding or any abdominal pain.'

Nothing I can do? Go to the hospital? I'm still getting comfortable with the idea of being pregnant. Now being not pregnant? For the first time, it occurs to me that this might go wrong.

'It would be a real shame...' Paul's voice trails off.

'We won't lose this...' What should I call it? I haven't allowed myself to think it's more than a bean-shaped lump of cells in my uterus; an ugly embryo the size of a blueberry, with remains of a tail, a rudimentary heart, tiny sprouts for arms and legs, and a brain that's growing one hundred thousand nerve cells every minute. It would be a real shame to lose this...

'...pregnancy,' I find the word. 'It'll be all right. You'll see.'

Days later, nausea with the special name of *morning sickness* lowers like fog, wafting in drifts, clouding my brain, confusing my emotions, knocking me flat.

Sleep, I can't get enough. Moods, I have in abundance. I'm in a tug-of-war between appetite and physiology, nausea and fatigue, discomfort and effort.

This body of mine is an alien thing. My sense of smell cranks to eleven on the dial. Appetite is fickle; gag reflex at the ready one minute, ravenously hungry the next. I can't brush my teeth without threatening to bring up breakfast.

The toilet is my new best friend. My expanding uterus is occupying more space than it used to. No matter what time of day, or how recently I peed, my bladder always feels full. That's not all. It seems the hormones that soften muscles and ligaments in anticipation of birth also affect the smooth muscles of the digestive tract, causing constipation. Fun. Not!

Procreation is a roller coaster. May as well let go and raise my hands.

June 1999

The week my morning sickness peaks, the Board of Education calls offering me a teaching contract shared between two primary schools in a sweet regional township in the mountains near Brisbane. It's the closest to full-time teaching work I've had since Japan. I can't afford to say no. The commute is manageable, so I agree to start immediately.

I keep my pregnancy a secret from colleagues. Most of my regular clothes still fit and winter layers conceal my changing shape. The deception isn't intentional. I just don't want anyone to treat me like yet another disappearing contract teacher, which I know I am. It doesn't take long before eyes in the staff room drift to my abdomen. Eventually, an older woman asks, 'My dear, are you expecting?'

I smile and nod coyly.

'Congratulations, love! We thought so. How far along are you?'

'Twenty weeks.'

'Goodness me, you're tiny!'

I look down at my belly. It doesn't seem tiny to me, but she isn't the first to say so.

'The hardest part is to come,' she continues. 'My doctor told me to scrub my nipples with a nail brush to toughen them up for breastfeeding.'

The staff room falls silent. My mouth falls open. The men all cough and look away. Another female teacher pipes up.

'They don't do that anymore, Vera.'

I'm relieved to hear it.

At home later that day, sitting cross-legged on the couch and spooning yoghurt from the tub, I feel a distinct poke on the inside. I stop eating and give it my attention. It happens again. I put down the yoghurt and splay my fingers wide on the surface of my belly so as not to miss a single sensation.

I feel it again, over and over in the same place. I look down – though there's nothing to see – and catch myself grinning. I have company. Intimate company. A tingle washes over me with an overwhelming sense of rightness in my body: this miracle that builds a unique person from just two cells. I was born with a lifetime of immature eggs in my ovaries. I'm built from a single cell that grew inside my mother when she was a foetus inside her mother: a cell bearing an ancient blueprint with a single purpose; to propel itself into the future.

'Hello, baby,' I whisper. The word no longer scares me. Incubating new life is a revelation akin to knowing God. I vow to sit with my baby often, hands to girth where I last detected movement, imagining the little person-becoming. What does it feel like to be in there, able to hear the outside world above the constant whoosh and gush of my heart and my guts? Can you feel me, little one? Who are you going to be? They say you can hear now and see light and dark. They even say that you dream. For all the little life you've had, floating there in inner space, what do you dream about?

That night, my thoughts flip over and I dream I'm a host for one of Giger's reptilian embryos that might suddenly claw its way from my insides, like in the movie. I oscillate between awe and excruciating doubt, and my dreams are weirder than Sigourney Weaver's because they're imbued with love.

At the end of the year, my contract ends, and my pregnancy means I won't be able to return. The school presents me with a farewell gift: a yellow baby blanket and a cute teddy bear.

Small compensation for a teaching career that never got started.

2 THE BEST JOB IN THE WORLD

December 2000

I exit the foyer of Maternity Outpatients at the Royal Women's Hospital; the sights and smells are familiar to me now. I take the elevator to the 3rd floor and continue walking along an enclosed gantry, more than fifty metres long and five stories above the ground. At the end, I arrive at level 5 of the Lady Ramsay building, housing ward M14, 15 and 17. The simple sign over conventional swinging doors states: Birth Centre.

The first thing you see when you enter is a confronting wall of birth photography. Naked women adorn the hallway, most of them at the moment of giving birth. Pendulous breasts with dark nipples. Blue-veined bellies with linea nigra. Pubic hair. Bodily fluids. Pink, blue, and purple just-born babies with a fatty film coating their bodies. Thank you cards and other ephemera give the eye relief, but you cannot unsee the wall.

Now in my third trimester, the pictures are like wallpaper. I understand there's a baby inside me that will have to come out. I sit down in the consultation room, tucking one hand under the weight of my belly. The other arm I present to Tamara, my midwife, for a blood pressure check.

She's jolly, as always. We're a good team. Both of us are keen photographers who love to travel. By some stroke of fate, our mobile phones have consecutive numbers and she's even the same age and star sign as me. She likes to talk – oh, how she talks! But I'll learn that, in labour, she listens.

With Tamara, nothing is secret or taboo. She talks about family in New Zealand, home renovations and her desire for a love life. She asks, 'How do I meet an eligible man while doing this job?'

I vent about the foibles of my pregnant body, nosebleeds, indigestion, achy hips, flatulence and constipation, without feeling that it's breaking an unspoken covenant. If I have questions, or feel scared, I can talk to her about it.

Tamara wraps my upper arm with the Velcro cuff and pumps the rubber bulb until my arm throbs. With a stethoscope to my inner elbow, she listens and releases the valve as the needle on the gauge drops to eighty. 'Blood pressure is perfect. Hop up on the bed and I'll measure your tummy.'

She helps me lie down on my back, which isn't so comfortable anymore, and loosens my clothing. She presses a tape measure into the fundus at the very top of my uterus – at home, I comfortably rest my coffee cup there – then pulls it taut over my protruding stomach to the ridge of the pelvic bone at my panty line. By some marvellous coincidence, centimetres roughly correspond to the week of pregnancy, making it easy to monitor a consistent rate of growth. Tamara explained all this to Paul and me at our initial appointment.

'Hm, tummy is still on the small side but you're a small person and Paul is a small person. I don't imagine you'll give birth to Goliath, do you?'

Mostly, I enjoy the compliments about my compact tummy. The thought of what a huge baby might do to my nether bits, quite frankly, scares me witless. Tamara writes something more than the measurement in my file.

Then she feels my belly with warm hands and prods the gap over my pelvic bone.

'Bub's still high and head down, as we'd expect.'

She feels along the sides of my stomach as the baby gives a resistant kick. Tamara pulls out the Doppler.

'I think we'll find the heartbeat right here.'

She places the sensor down low on my tummy and immediately the speaker unit in her hand emits a bloop-bloop-bloop. I grin so wide my eyes water. She lets me listen until I get restless, then packs it away.

'Do you have any plans for New Year?'

'Paul's on call for Y2K, so we thought we might hang out on the balcony at his workplace in Milton. We can see the Southbank fireworks from there. Am I allowed to have a glass of champagne?'

'It's not recommended,' she winks, 'but I doubt one glass will hurt.' She helps me sit up and straighten my clothes. 'I'll be on night shift, so think of me when the clock strikes midnight.'

'How unlucky can you get?'

She laughs. 'It's all right. Babies always arrive on public holidays, don't you know? I've a client due Christmas Day and another due New Year's Day. Both want the trophy for *first baby of the new millennium*. I fully expect one of them will be in labour New Year's Eve.'

I'm disappointed for her. 'Well, don't work too hard.'

'Believe me, this isn't my idea of hard work. Here,' she hands me a clear plastic specimen jar with a yellow lid, 'can you pee?'

I take it in my hand. 'I can always pee...'

January 2000

At my next visit, around thirty-five weeks gestation, Tamara measures my belly.

'Have you been feeling lots of movement?' she asks, draping the tape measure around her neck like a dressmaker.

'Oh yes, active as ever.'

'Your tummy measures about the same as last week, and not much more than the week before.' She doesn't seem alarmed. I peek at my file where she's writing 'IUGR?' At home I consult the almighty internet. IntraUterine Growth Restriction is a threatening acronym, but the question mark gives me hope.

'Clever you,' Tamara says at the next week's appointment when I present her with what I've learned. 'You did some research, so you'll understand why I'm referring you to Foetal Medicine.' And, like that, I step onto a carousel of weekly scans and foetal stress tests to monitor the baby's well-being until it's time to be born.

February 2000

My mother has offered to help for a few weeks, so Dad chauffeurs her down from the Sunshine Coast. They arrive at our door three days before my official due date and greet me with a hug and a lot of fuss. Mum has stopped dyeing her hair and the grey shimmer flatters her skin tones. Dad, who's bald like every man in the Smithfield family, shakes Paul's hand and they congratulate each other, unsure how to play their new roles.

'It's about time you made us grandparents,' Mum jokes, not for the first time.

'We aim to please,' Paul shoots back, with just a hint of tension.

After a quick cup of tea, Dad announces he'll be on his way home. We stand in the doorway and wave him off.

I turn to Mum, 'I think I'm leaking.'

Her face goes white and her mouth moves, but no words come.

Paul suggests I call Tamara. Within an hour we're at the Birth Centre and I'm strapped to the foetal heart monitor. Tanya swabs me and squints at the colour chart.

'Yep, it's amniotic fluid. Probably what we call a hind leak, a tear in the membranes. They're still intact and bub is plugging the leak for now. You'll make more fluid to replace what you lose, so don't worry. His heart rate is fine. He's perfectly happy in there.'

Policy dictates that I have 36 hours to go into labour naturally, and I must consent to antibiotics via a cannula in the back of my hand or lose access to the Birth Centre. The consultant obstetrician suggests that we make an appointment for an induction now, rather than let it escalate to a complication when her schedule is full. I feel like they're assuming the worst. Whatever else I do now, I must prioritise going into labour. Like it's a choice?

Lucky for me, it's Sunday and the hospital is operating on a weekend roster. Monday is solidly booked, so the obstetrician schedules our baby's induction for first thing Tuesday morning. When she's gone, I reach for Paul's hand and turn to Tamara.

'We can still use the Birth Centre, can't we?' I had become rather attached to the idea of the tub, maybe even giving birth in the water. My imagined first night with Paul in the double bed with our baby swaddled cosy between us is replaced by Paul sleeping in a recliner beside my hospital bed, or worse, at home alone, and our baby in one of those impersonal Perspex cradles in the nursery. Tamara beckons us up the hall, past the wall of birth photography, to the common room.

'They'll have to induce you in the labour ward,' she says, 'but once labour's established, you can come back to the Birth Centre, just like we planned.'

I panic a little, 'They say an induced labour's more painful.'

'Here's the thing: you're at term. Bub's doing fine. You've met the first step leading to your baby's arrival. Booking your induction is just a formality. Hospital policy.'

'Do I have to be induced?'

She puts a comforting hand on my arm. 'It's policy, not law. You can decline to be induced, and all going well, you may not need it. I'll find you some information.'

We stop at the resource library in the common room. There's a brass plate on the cabinet that reads *Donated by Friends of the Birth Centre*. Tamara opens the glass door and runs her hand over a bank of ring binders until she finds the right one. She extracts it and opens to a coloured tab, and from a clear plastic sleeve she pulls some photocopied pages.

'These are recent and from reputable journals. Read them and discuss with Paul. Call me at any time.' She hands me a wad of articles on Rupture Of Membranes.

'And this,' she plucks another page titled Informed Consent.

'And here,' she flicks through a bank of business cards in a little rack on the bookshelf and offers one to me. 'This acupuncturist treats a lot of clients from the Birth Centre. Let's see if we can't get things moving before Tuesday, hm?'

I take the card feebly and look at Paul with no idea what acupuncture can do for me.

Tamara walks us to the elevator, shakes Paul's hand formally and gives me a big hug. With a wink she says, 'See you soon.'

A hot curry and six acupuncture needles later, I lie in bed in the dark of night. One juicy saddle contraction grabs my attention. It pulls from my groin, down my inner thighs. Nothing more. Booking the induction has given this pregnancy a deadline but feeling the first mild pain of labour suddenly makes everything terrifyingly real. Will I be capable of giving birth? Will I be different afterwards?

'You okay?' Half asleep, Paul spoons me on our futon while a pedestal fan blows hot air over us. My mother sleeps in the room next door.

'Ready or not,' I whisper, blinking back tears, 'tomorrow we're having a baby.'

'We're ready,' yawns Paul. 'I installed the baby capsule today.' He rolls over and soon his breathing is slow and regular. I stare at the wall, unable to heed the advice to sleep while I can. I'm not prepared. I was counting on a burst of nesting energy.

The baby's room still isn't ready. I was hoping for a chance to bond with Mum over curtains and comforters.

Valentine's Day 2000

It's a few days before my due date and we dutifully drive to the hospital for the induction. I can't feel them, but Tamara identifies gentle, regular contractions, fifteen minutes apart. To my great relief, all parties agree we should go home and let nature take its course.

On the car ride home, Paul seems worried, but a feeling of immense calm washes over me, with a small flutter of excitement in the undercurrent. The contractions continue all day, mildly uncomfortable, but I can walk and talk and carry on with my day to day. If this is all there is to deal with, everything will be just fine.

Around 5 pm, the contractions come in waves and start to bite. I hug a heat pack to my belly and pace a circuit around our home, from kitchen to courtyard to hallway and back, then start all over again. Paul keeps reminding me that's one less contraction I have to endure, and it works until I have a sudden urge to vomit. After that, the pains become so intense I can no longer talk through them.

'I want to see Tamara, right now,' I gasp. Paul makes the call.

He drives me to the hospital while I hug a bucket, and we arrive at the Birth Centre around 8 pm. Tamara is filling the tub. The lights are dim. The room is warm, and the atmosphere is welcoming.

'Where is everyone?' I ask in a moment of reprieve. Tamara's smile is broad as she unstraps the foetal monitor from my belly, hopefully for the last time.

'We had a run of babies over the weekend. Everyone went home today. We have the whole place to ourselves! Settle in and get comfortable. Tonight, you get to meet your baby.'

I put my favourite CD in the stereo, turn it down low, and continue to pace the floor, breathing deeply through contractions. Hours pass. My face and teeth and fingertips tingle. Nothing can distract me from the sensations in my belly, my thighs, my lower back, my undercarriage. I autopilot a routine of pacing, crouching, breathing, and breaking to pee until fatigue taps my shoulder and Tamara suggests a different dance.

Paul offers his hand and helps me into the tub. I don't know where I am anymore, or where this labour is at. Am I making progress? How much longer can I endure this? Will it be hours more or mere minutes? Please tell me we're getting close! I sink to my neck in deep warm water: the midwife's epidural. In my mind's eye, I'm clothed in luxuriant velvet, held like a baby, floating weightless in the womb-tub. All my doubts melt away and for a few moments, I merge with my surroundings and cease to exist.

'You're doing great, Jodie. Not long now,' Tamara encourages me to keep moving and find a position that makes the pain endurable. I make some involuntary noises and am embarrassed by the sexual sound of my growls, but Tamara says to go with it. For want of trying, I don't know how to push. Tamara directs me to push into my bottom and I guess I knew I got it right by pushing out a floater.

Is this not every woman's nightmare? I've never so much as peed in front of Paul. Tamara declares it a good sign and removes it with a plastic sieve to be flushed. She returns with a mirror and a Dolphin torch and directs light into my vagina, telling me she can see the baby's hair and I can put my hand down and feel it, which I do, but I can't identify where my body ends and baby begins. Paul leans in and says, 'Thank you for having our baby.' It's the burst of love I need to slow down and breathe the baby out.

Words are alien to my consciousness, but I manage an, 'Owowow!' The baby's head is stretching me, a circle of red-hot fire. It lasts an eternity.

'You're nearly there,' Tamara coaxes. 'At the next contraction, I want you to give one long push.'

'I can't. I'm scared!'

'You can do it, Jodie. Women do it every day.'

Women do it every day. Suddenly, I'm not alone. In a haze of endorphins, I fantasise that hundreds of thousands of women in the world are pushing out their babies with me. Ghosts of my ancestors encircle the room and as the next contraction builds, because Tamara wants me to, I bear down one more time. At the point of maximum stretch, when I fear I might split open and die giving life, an involuntary screech escapes my throat, and a head arrives underwater with a visceral pop. Sweet relief.

I can see the back of my baby's head, like a hairy ball the size of an orange, protruding from my pubes. I know that he's safe and won't breathe until his skin meets the air, but it's a weird and wonderful limbo, this extended spell with no contractions, not-yet-born. I feel Paul, who sits behind me on the edge of the tub, wiping a stray hair from my face. My awareness returns. Tamara puts the mirror on the bottom of the tub so I can see our baby's squishy little face.

One more push and, not long after midnight, the rest of him is born into the warm water of the jacuzzi tub. In one motion, Tamara guides the baby through the water and up to my chest where he gurgles and cries and then immediately calms. My fatigue evaporates. I love him the instant I touch him, this divine creature, waxy cone head, red skin, hairy arms, long fingernails and all. 6lb 2oz, small but alert and ready to be born.

Paul got his wish. He's a daddy now. I'm yet to join the cult of motherhood, but later, the night we get home from the Birth Centre, while bub sleeps beside us in his bassinet, we make love, sweetly and innocently. My postpartum body is too tender for intercourse, so we kiss, and we fumble, and we celebrate ourselves. How many new mothers do that, I wonder, so soon after giving birth? Can this kind of joy exist without the agony that came before?

Two weeks later I muster the courage to submit our photo film for processing. We'd entrusted our camera to a stranger, a midwife from the wards witnessing her first waterbirth. With only six or seven frames left on the reel, I've no idea what to expect. I open the envelope of black and white prints and fan them out discreetly. I don't have to be afraid. Their raw, sensual beauty takes my breath away. The expressions of my face offer no distinction between pleasure and pain. For years to come, I'll see these pictures and return to that womb-like space. Now I understand the photos lining the walls of the Birth Centre. They represent layers of experience. They normalise birth for new mothers like me and help dispel the fear. I want to do that for others too.

I give duplicates to Tamara saying, 'You have the best job in the world!'

3 LEGACY

March 2000

I loved Elijah instantly. His smell is intoxicating, but I don't have a clue what to do. It's Paul who changes the first tar-like nappy, gives Elijah his first bath, and paces the floor to raise a gaseous bubble from his immature belly.

I'd put all my preparation into giving birth and barely gave a thought to life with a newborn. The sound of his crying is torment, but I don't know how to soothe him. What am I doing wrong? I have plenty of milk and he's gaining weight. I doubt my actions every single moment. Mum says she's never known a baby to cry so much, offering the usual suggestions: swaddling, dummies, long walks, warm baths, massage. We try it all.

My breasts have become a separate entity, detached from my corporal body. I get 'let-downs', meaning my full and veiny boobs tingle and the nipples burn like an ice cube left on the skin too long; then before I know it, electric shocks deliver two wet patches to my shirt front. It can strike anytime: while driving, or catching a cool breeze that gives you goose bumps, or watching someone else breastfeed, or cradling a loaf of bread in the queue at the supermarket, and always at the sound of a baby's cry, even on TV. A visiting friend hugged me hard, not realising how much it hurt, and stepped away with my wet patches.

There's no rest. Completing one feed fills me with dread for the next. Chin to chest, babe to breast. Repeat. I'm the baby, weepy and fragile. I need my mother and Paul to cook, remind me to drink water, calm me down when the crying triggers me. We've come this close to buying a tin of formula, but somehow baby and I find our groove before I lose my mind.

My darkest days are delivered like a shroud. Paul returns to work and Mum goes home. I'm a helpless newborn mother, home alone, recklessly entrusted with the wellbeing of a tiny human. I'm scared witless.

Elijah cries himself to sleep. He cries himself awake too – just picks up where he left off, usually in my arms because putting him down risks waking him again. Every afternoon around four o'clock he screams inconsolably for at least an hour before collapsing into a fitful sleep. He wakes hungry every other hour, day and night.

I dutifully bounce him, rock him, pat him. My tension makes it worse. His cries increase in pitch and urgency, his little face goes red. Tears brim my eyes and I can hardly see. I want to scream. Suddenly there's the irrepressible urge to shake him, hard. Anything to stop this crying!

I catch my breath, put him down as gently as I can, and step back in shock. I block my ears to his crying and take some deep breaths. I visit the bathroom to splash water on my face and I see my reflection in the mirror. Dark circles, worry lines, ratty hair, milk stains on my shirt. Who's this person?

I don't trust myself to be alone with the baby, so I call for backup.

'Paul?' There's no time for hellos. 'Can you leave early?'

'It's four o'clock. I'll be home around six.' Can't he hear Elijah howling in the next room? Doesn't he know I wouldn't be asking if I wasn't batshit crazy and worried I might hurt our baby?

'I can't do this,' I snivel, 'I need you. Please?'

'Okay, I'm coming.'

I whimper a thank you and hang up the phone. What am I going to do for the 30 minutes before he gets home? Somehow it passes and when Paul arrives, flustered but ready for duty, I wordlessly hand over the baby and disappear for a long shower, a hard cry, and a short spell of rocking in a corner.

I present at mothers' group with nothing to lose. I need to know that other first-timers are having the same hardships as me. It's reassuring to learn that they cry as much, wake as often, feed as frequently. I feel a pang of jealousy when one mother declares that her baby slept through the night. Elijah still wakes on a two-hourly cycle. What a hopeless mother I am!

Grief visits often in the silence at midnight. I can't shut it out in the darkness. I haven't slept more than a two-hour stretch since Elijah was born. I compulsively monitor his night-time gurgles for fear he might become a SIDS statistic.

Paul reaches over in the night-time, to stroke my hair. I know what it means. How dare he. Sex is the last thing on my mind, especially with our baby in the room. My body is alien. Everything leaks. It's hard to feel sexy. Is it like this for all new mothers, or is it just me?

February 2001

Learning to be Elijah's mother has been the hardest, most selfless thing I've ever done. Through a triage of teething and fevers and baby boy bumps, scrapes, and first steps, I emerge from my shroud. Elijah, still doesn't sleep through the night, still falls asleep in my arms, but my yearning to backpack Asia has subsided to a gentle resignation that having babies can be rewarding too.

Paul throws the mail on the kitchen bench and gestures with his hands *shall I take him*? I nod and hand Elijah over. Our synergy is the subtle love Paul and I pass back and forth, wordlessly pre-empting each other's needs. I rarely have to ask for anything. He anticipates my thirst with a glass of water, my appetite with a protein snack, my fatigue with a sweet cup of tea. It's our special brand of magic.

'Your newsletter is in there,' Paul says as he takes Elijah to his cot.

I put on the kettle and flick through the envelopes. We joined Friends of the Birth Centre – FBC for short – once I found the social support of my mothers' group. Those women are my new tribe. They give me a reason to leave the house and are still my lifeline in those moments when I think I might drown in self-pity. I don't know how working mother's cope. Even a year later I feel nowhere near ready to return to the classroom. I'd be half the teacher, and half the mother, and dissatisfied with my performance in both.

The FBC newsletter, *Special Delivery*, comes out quarterly and I read it from cover to cover. It's a conduit to a political world of motherhood that's completely new to me. After Elijah was born there was a six month 'waterbirth ban' while the hospital conducted a review, a ban the Birth Centre advocates considered unnecessary. Sometimes there are articles about global maternity news, like the findings of the *Term Breech Trial*. A randomised control trial has apparently proven that vaginal breech births are more dangerous than caesarean section, so hospitals have stopped conducting them. But the politics is peripheral. Two or three detailed birth stories appear in every issue and I never tire of them. Often, I re-read them as a reminder of the wonder of it all.

I hold up the page advertising the FBC Annual General Meeting.

'Should I go? It's next month.'

'I'll mind Elijah,' Paul replies.

'What kind of people do you think they are?' I imagine radical, leftie women, braless, with hairy armpits.

'There's only one way to find out,' he smiles.

We're having a small party for Elijah's first birthday, with banana bread in lieu of cake. Friends from mothers' group are coming. Their babies have also turned one. I'm feeling more in command of my world now Elijah can almost walk and talk, and his personality is beginning to blossom. But I feel a bit 'off' and I can't explain it. I don't recognise the weirdness, the dreams, the emotional meltdowns, the desire to cut my hair. This nausea, I'm sure, is a tummy bug. I've just weaned Elijah and had only one period since he was born.

Before everyone arrives, I take a pregnancy test. The result is instantaneous. I could be as much as eight weeks along. Paul is delighted. Naturally, I call my dear midwife, Tamara. She says she'll add my name to the Birth Centre ballot. I couldn't contemplate having a baby with anyone else.

Finally, I call my mother.

4 ECHOES

April 2001

Tamara calls to announce that my name was drawn, and I've acquired a place at the Birth Centre. She has nominated to be my midwife. I'm relieved. With places so limited, how disappointing it must be to miss out and return to a random doctor or midwife at every appointment, having the same conversation with a new care provider over and over, and a stranger on shift when I go into labour. I don't think I could do that, knowing what I know now.

I progress from reading *Special Delivery* to attending the AGM for Friends of the Birth Centre at a lovely old home on a busy junction in Ashgrove. In the kitchen, over a cup of tea, I meet a soft-spoken woman called Kareena. Her partner Brendan bounces their daughter in his arms. I lean in and greet them rather too formally.

'Nice to meet you too,' says Kareena. 'This is Tilly. She's one.'

I blurt, 'I've a one-year-old, at home with my husband.' And because I can't let another presence go unacknowledged, I pat my belly, 'And one on the way.'

'Congratulations!' Kareena says. 'Did you get into the Birth Centre?'

'Thankfully, yes.'

'I'm not sure I'm ready to go again. Can't use the Birth Centre. Tilly was a caesarean in the end.'

'What do you mean?' My voice is shrill.

'They don't allow it,' Kareena whispers because the meeting is about to start. 'You have to be low risk for the Birth Centre. A scar automatically excludes me.'

'But the Birth Centre is in a hospital,' I'm whispering too. 'A hospital that does organ transplants and stuff. Surely just wanting a normal birth makes you an ideal candidate for the Birth Centre?'

'You would think so.' She shrugs her shoulders with regret. I'm sure decision-makers at the Royal have justifiable reasons, but I'm disappointed for her.

The meeting begins. A new president is elected, treasury reports are delivered and there is a discussion about a Baby Goods Sale. I'm not really into that, but I commit to attending a members' meeting. No one was braless. No unusual hair either. Just regular new mothers and fathers living the chaos of young family life; sleep deprivation, multi-tasking, juggling nap times and potty trips, short attention spans and all.

It's an opportunity to meet other people at this stage of life, and to work my teacher brain. I offer to generate some value for members in the form of a wall planner, paid for by sponsors offering discounts to the FBC members. It feels good to be doing something other than being a wife and mother.

September 2001

Without all the novelty of the first time around, my pregnancy progresses effortlessly and less wondrously. My belly, at eight months, is larger than it was when Elijah was born. Today my plans are simple. I'll take Elijah to the sitter so I can visit the printer to examine the final proof before the wall planner goes to print. I switch on the TV to catch a snippet of the morning news before heading out the door.

But today is different. Unbelievably, a hijacked passenger plane has flown into the North Tower of the World Trade Centre in New York. Twenty minutes later another plane hit the South Tower. With both towers on fire and many lives lost, the first tower collapsed while evacuations were underway. Another plane has crashed into the Pentagon in Washington. The baby kicks me in furious distress. At 7.20 am in Brisbane, Australia, I weep in real-time with the collapse of the second towering inferno. I forget to eat breakfast and take Elijah to the sitter and see the printer. I cannot function today. We're on the cusp of World War Three and in less than a month I'm due to bring a new life into this ugly world.

October 2001

I close my eyes and breathe against a rising sense of panic. That last contraction made me sick to my stomach.

I heave into the porcelain toilet in the shiny new Birth Centre. It has only been open a matter of months. It feels like home though, since all my recent appointments have been in these rooms, with Tamara keeping things normal and familiar. I groan as another contraction starts before the previous one has ended. There's a subtle pop low in my pelvis and a trickle of warmth runs down my leg. I grip the wall, knees shaking. Inhale…exhale.

Tamara calls through the bathroom door, 'How are you going in there?'

'Okay,' I huff. 'I think my waters broke.'

I turn towards the sink, splash my face, rinse my mouth, check myself in the mirror. Who's this woman, all sweaty and flushed? Pupils dilated. Mouth open. Hair dishevelled. Naked from the waist down.

My reflection flirts with me. Fuck I look sexy!

The rumblings begin anew. Contractions pull like elastic hooks in the muscles of my inner thighs, up through my pelvis and into my navel and lower back. They command all my attention. My belly forms a hard shell. An involuntary moan crescendo as I try to contain the power, slow things down, hold it in. But I can't. The tidal force gives me no choice but to surrender and let it sweep me away.

When the contraction has subsided, I know the baby has shifted. Calm returns. Inhale...exhale.

I get ready for another wave. Sure enough, it swells and comes crashing to shore. Gripping the bathroom sink, the goddess in the mirror roars at me.

'I wanna puuuu~sh!'

'Breathe,' Tamara appears at the door and extends her hand for me to grasp. Her energy reassures me.

'The bath is full, come on in.' She helps me peel off my shirt and guides me naked toward the tub.

I clutch for Paul, who takes my hand with a look of love and I step once more into deep, warm water. Fatigue and nausea pass. For a moment I exist in the eye of a storm. I reserve some energy for the effort ahead.

Another contraction is building. It's happening so much faster this time. I close my eyes, squeeze Paul's hand, brace my feet against the tub and bear down with all my primal might. A howl echoes around the room like it came from somewhere else. This time, no one has to tell me how to push.

A familiar burning stretch between my legs reminds me to slow down, take my time, let it happen, don't force. I pant and clutch my thighs, desperate not to feel my body splitting in two. I hear myself screech and know what comes next.

A purple bulb protrudes from my body underwater, visible through the ripples like a surrealist painting. Tamara puts a mirror on the bottom of the bath so I can see her face. I feel composed again and take a moment to rest.

'Get your hands ready, Jodie,' she urges. I realise I'm waiting for permission to catch my baby.

One more push. With a twist of her shoulders and a kick in my diaphragm, our second child ejects herself into my hands. I lift her from the water, and she declares her arrival with a lusty cry. Instantly pink, fragile, and slippery, I fumble her to my chest.

'I did it.' Words spoken like a child. Paul kisses me. The second midwife takes photos. We all drink in her newness.

'Hello, baby girl. Welcome to the world.'

The alchemy that triggered that first contraction, ending a nine-month metamorphosis, reaches its final stage as she nurses reflexively, like she's been here before. Contraction, placenta, relocate to the bed. The midwives swaddle me and my baby, naked together, skin on skin. Paul snuggles in close.
More pictures. Instant family. I feel euphoric.

And this time I know how lucky I am. Birth is not like this for everyone.

My 'boggy' uterus doesn't want to shrink back, despite a suckling baby. Tamara asks for consent to give me a shot of artificial oxytocin and my insides snap back like an elastic band. Aside from feeling crampy, and woozy on my feet, it's wonderful to share the double bed with Paul: baby Ruby nestled between us. We both know what to do and the midwives leave us to ourselves. The next morning, they say I'm well enough for discharge with a promise that I'll rest in bed, lift nothing heavier than my baby, eat lots of fibre, and drink lots of water.

We arrive home around ten o'clock. Mum greets us with Elijah, now 20 months old, on her hip, still in his pyjamas. She puts him down so he can run to us. We goo and gaa at our new addition. Elijah's eyes sparkle, wide and bright.

'Baby,' he says.

'Yes, baby sister. What do you think, Elijah?'

'Lovely!' He looks up with a coy expression and then leans in and kisses her head.

'And who are you?' asks Paul.

'Big brother!' he shouts and jumps and wobbles with excitement. His toddler ecstasy fills the room. We're home.

Mum insists we put Elijah and Ruby together on the couch for the obligatory sibling photo. Dad will be here soon to take her home. She'll return in a month when Paul begins his taxing pre-Christmas 'around the world' trip, visiting the global offices and engaging with his staff. It takes three gruelling weeks to visit five locations in four time zones. Communication between us will be difficult. So Mum will come the weekend after Paul leaves. I'm dreading the few days I'll have to cope alone with both children, but at the same time, I'm ready to test myself. Have I learned anything? Can I manage for three days?

Turns out, I can.

It delights Mum to have another grandchild, now a pigeon pair! She flutters from room to room, keeping herself busy and urging me to sleep, even though I've not napped since I was a toddler myself. She occupies Elijah while I change Ruby's nappies, feed her and pat her off to sleep. She happily cuddles Ruby so I can enjoy some shower and toilet time alone – small luxuries like this keep me sane. Baby and I have a better rhythm this time. And perhaps I've gained some patience.

If I'm objective, I think Ruby cries almost as much and wakes almost as often as her older brother did. The difference this time is me. The sound of a crying baby doesn't turn me so inside out anymore. I can ride it out. I'm calmer.

Now that Elijah is in a bed, I put Ruby in the cot. She usually sleeps until about 1 am, when I bring her to our bed, and she stays the rest of the night with me. The sun is up and Ruby stirs, so we breastfeed. Mum greets me at the door with a lovely cup of tea.

'You're awake?'

'Yes, what time is it?' I yawn.

'A little after seven.' In my world, that qualifies as a sleep-in.

'I heard Elijah. How often did you get up last night?' Mum is a light sleeper. She probably knows.

'Not sure,' I say, which is true. I've long ceased counting, or even caring. It hurts my mental health to dwell on it. I don't judge the night. It is what it is.

'I breastfed you for ten months, and you slept through from six weeks,' Mum asserts, not for the first time. 'You were such a good baby.'

The skin prickles on the back of my neck. I had expected Elijah to sleep through to the same timeline and was bitterly disappointed. He's almost two and still wakes often. Is there anything I haven't done to promote healthy sleep? I'm grateful for Mum, but Paul never presents me with an ideal that's drastically different from my reality. I decide not to care. Whatever she remembers may not be how it was.

'Does this go here?'

The familiar prickles return. Mum has been here for two weeks. She's unstacking the dishwasher while I snuggle a sleeping baby. The cycle only just finished. Please, can't she rest? Yesterday we sorted the linen cupboard and washed all the sheets. The day before, she wiped the walls and gave the floors a mop. I'm holding her back from sorting the pantry. Her energy makes me tense.

'Thanks, Mum, that's enough.'

'I'm only helping, Jodie.'

'It's okay to leave it, really.'

Truth is, I'd rather do it myself. Elijah and Ruby and I are falling into a comfortable rhythm. Mum is crowding me. A few days alone with the children would be nice before Paul gets home.

'You don't want me to help?' She's sweeping the floor now, though there isn't a crumb I can see.

'Let's sit down and just talk' I don't remember her being this agitated when Elijah was born, but Paul was around to diffuse the tension.

'Talk? About what?'

Mum stacks the broom in the corner and proceeds to hover over Elijah. She supervises him with the same script from my childhood.

'Don't fall!' 'You'll cut yourself!' 'Ouch! Hot! Burnie!' 'Stop that!'

I enjoy having Mum chit-chatting, recounting her stories of motherhood that I previously gave no mind. Her own childhood seemed to lack love and attention. Being the poorest family in the neighbourhood left a scar. As the eleventh of twelve children, by then only eight remained at home, sleeping two to a bed in a three-bedroom house. By the time she was 14, all her older siblings had left. At 15, Mum left too, to live with her newlywed sister. Why would the youngest daughter leave home so young?

Mum rarely ever let her children out of her sight. I never felt like I could, or should, do adventurous things like go camping with Dad and my brother. Or later, go on dates, or drive in cars with boys.

I tiptoe away and put Ruby down in her cot, closing the door to a crack so I can still hear her stir.

'Let's watch a movie.' This is how I engage Mum in 'together time'.

'Okay.' She pulls out her DVD file. 'Shirley Valentine?' Mum holds up the disk for me to see.

I resist asking, 'How many times has it been?' and manage a more neutral, 'Sure, why not?'

She loves this movie. Originally a one-woman stage show, it became a liberation movie for middle-aged women. The protagonist leaves Liverpool, her husband and family, for a holiday in Greece where she finds joy and eventually makes it her home. It's a little naff for my taste, but what the heck! Let's relax and have fun.

The kettle babbles and shuts itself off. I put leaves in a pot with two mugs and a jug of milk on the tray, cheese and crackers, and some sliced apple. We settle in. Elijah snacks while he plays with trucks and blocks on the floor.

By the time the credits roll, we both see what he's doing. He has stacked his blocks in two tall towers and is mock-flying around them with a toy airplane. It's spooky. The terrorist attack was almost three months ago but It's still often in the news. I look at Mum, my question clear. Does he really remember that? Suddenly he lunges and demolishes a stack of blocks with the plane in his hand. I catch my breath and lean in, 'What are you doing Elijah?'

'Knock dem down,' he knocks down the second tower, then rams the plane in my face.

Mum bounds from her chair and slaps the plane from Elijah's hand.

'Elijah, no! Naughty!'

I'm mortified. 'Mum, he doesn't know any better!'

I lock eyes with my mother for a moment, reliving a distant memory. In 1973, I was three years old. Not every house had a telephone. Mum used to climb the waist-high fence to our neighbour's place and ask to use their phone. I'd followed her, leaving my baby brother unsupervised on a blanket on the floor. I'd returned to four strikes of her leather sandal, delivered to my raw backside in time with her reprimand:

'I TOLD you NOT to LEAVE your BROTHER!' I'd opened my mouth wide and howled from the sting of it.

Elijah freezes and looks at both of us, confused. Then opens his mouth wide and howls.

Mum's eyes soften. She hugs the uncomprehending Elijah. He'll be okay, of course, but the ghosts of our past sometimes ooze like bubbles from the muck. Every time I admonish Elijah, I hear her voice come out of me. 'I told you not to…' from when a clip over the ear, or a slap on the leg, was felt before you knew what you had done to deserve it.

5 FRIENDS

March 2002

Rebecca is in her second year as president of Friends of the Birth Centre. Meetings at her house are comfortable because there's space for all the children to play. The open plan design means we can sit around the snacks on her generous table and supervise our little ones across the room. Everything is contained, and that's peace of mind for a mother.

Breast feeders score the comfy couch beside the play area. Pregnant women and mothers of newborns are waited on by those with independent children. It's unspoken, the natural order of things. If Paul is away, I bring Elijah, but it's usually just me and Ruby. She's five months old and happy on a blanket on the floor, on my lap, or bouncing on my hip. Rebecca's husband usually makes himself scarce, although he works behind the scenes administrating a website for FBC.

Bec calls the room to order. She waits for the hum to settle, 'Great to see so many of you here. Did you get tea or coffee? It's been a big month so let's get started.'

We're the new generation Friends of the Birth Centre, or 'FBC'. When Elijah was ten months old, I'd bought him a tiny FBC t-shirt declaring, in comic sans: A Midwife Helped Me Out. It's been a source of amused conversation with strangers ever since. Some babies wear theirs today.

Bec has a daughter about two years old. Emma is the FBC secretary, a single mum with a toddler son, and the most office-skilled person here. Along with the long-standing Treasurer, they ebb and flow with the synergy of a good team.

'Incoming correspondence,' Emma interjects, pencil poised over her minutes. The room falls silent but for the sound of child's play and the eternal drone of the television.

Bec coughs and holds up a page with letterhead. 'From Bruce Teakle of the Brisbane Birth Action Group regarding NMAP.' She pronounces it N-map which I know is the *National Maternity Action Plan*. It's a white paper, developed by Dr Barbara Vernon, and augmented by Dr Tracy Reibel, and Dr Sally Tracy, pitching primary midwifery care as a solution to safe and cost-effective maternity services under Medicare in Australia. That's the case in New Zealand, and the UK, where many of the Birth Centre midwives trained. The Netherlands is similar, too.

Rebecca summarises the letter, 'Bruce is requesting that families accompany him to visit their local Member of Parliament. All you have to do is talk about your experience at the Birth Centre. Bruce will then explain the potential of NMAP in the context of Medicare, including rural and remote locations.' She puts the page down, giving us time to digest the request.

A murmur builds around the table. The world is still reeling from 9/11. Prior to that, several insurance agencies had collapsed, including one of Australia's largest. Obstetrics is a specialisation particularly prone to litigation, and hospitals are risk-averse places. Skyrocketing premiums have prompted GPs and surgeons to sign assets over to their families, or a family trust, so that if a patient should sue for malpractice, they won't lose their family home.

They say doctors get sued for the timely caesarean they didn't do. The only thing worse than losing a mother or baby is leaving one, or both, injured for life. A recent compensation case awarded an unprecedented 14 million dollars to a girl born with cerebral palsy – the most common result of a childbirth accident. Since care providers in the maternity space can be sued up to 18 years after the fact, midwives and obstetricians must maintain insurance long beyond retirement. The insurance collapse left privately practising midwives without an option for professional indemnity, ending their visiting rights to hospitals and destroying the safety net of their businesses.

Rebecca finishes. 'So, let's get behind Bruce and contact our local MPs. He's asking us to make an appointment, then invite him to attend.'

We all say we will but aren't exactly falling over ourselves to make the call. We live in our white, middle-class, university-educated bubble, advocating for the Birth Centre. What can NMAP do for us?

Rebecca moves on to the next agenda item, the bake stall in the new hospital foyer is a reliable fund raiser, and then there's the birthday party held every June for the anniversary of the Birth Centre. It's time to choose a date and venue.

I squirm in my chair. I can't see myself volunteering to bake brownies or conduct a raffle. My little wall planner project gave me purpose when I was feeling swallowed by motherhood. I've nominated to do the next one too, and more.

Rebecca is a midwife on maternity leave from the Royal. Since joining FBC I've been relentless with my questions; about the Birth Centre, midwifery practice, and the professional organisations that govern the field. Bec couldn't answer them all so she told me to join an email list, *Ozmidwifery*, started by a childbirth educator and midwife.

'This,' she'd said, 'will answer all of your questions. There's lots of jargon, but consumers are welcome to observe and participate.'

Bec brings us all back on track. She raises her voice a notch so the mamas on the couch can hear.

'You probably all know that my maternity leave will be over soon. Next month is the Annual General Meeting and I'm giving notice now that I'll not be renominating.'

Save for the TV and the raucous toddlers, the room falls silent. A lone voice expresses an objection.

'I know,' she raises her hand, 'but I'm going back to work and as an employee of the hospital, FBC is a conflict of interest. It's in the Code of Conduct. I can't do both.'

I'm clueless about bureaucracy. Where else does a consumer group advocate for both sides of the agenda: the consumers of a service and the providers of that service?

'Which is why…' she waits until the room grows quiet, 'I nominate Jodie to replace me.' She looks directly at me with her soft brown eyes and asks, 'Is this okay?'

'But I haven't got a clue about any of it.'

'You'll pick it up,' she says. 'We play together well. You've got the spunk and curiosity for the job. You'll be fine.'

Her compliments belie the fact that I've no relevant experience or skills with committees or financial governance. The idea of liaising with the hospital fills me with terror. But these women have become friends, as have the Birth Centre midwives. I would jump from an airplane for them.

There are noises of support from the rest of the room and I'm suddenly inspired.

'I've got nothing to lose,' I reply.

What am I going to tell Paul? He didn't sign up for this.

'Daddy! Daddy!' Elijah squeals as a taxi pulls into our driveway.

Ruby crawls at lightning speed towards the door. She mimics her brother with a 'da da da'. I pick her up and we congregate in the front yard, waiting for Paul to pay the driver, collect his bags and re-enter our lives. Dropping his luggage on the footpath, he comes toward us, scooping Elijah up in his arms.

'It's sooo good to see you,' I collect Ruby from the floor to my hip and receive a much-anticipated kiss from my beloved. He hugs us all in a bundle.

'I missed you too,' he sighs. 'Here,' he puts Elijah back down on his feet and returns to his bag, 'I've got presents!'

Inside the house, the ritual suitcase inspection reveals some duty-free beauty products for me, a tiny Massachusetts t-shirt for Elijah and a teddy bear for Ruby.

I read Paul's weary face. He returns my gaze with a confessional expression.

'I'm back next month. The CEO will visit engineering. It's a last-minute thing.'

This is our life now. Paul's a willing provider and the burden of our mortgage is shrinking. I'm grateful that among what causes us friction, money doesn't count. But I always, always get my hopes up when Paul gets home. I'll have an adult to talk to, someone to share the parenting load. Finally, I can have an uninterrupted shower. And after three unrefreshed weeks of toddler duty, a meal I didn't have to prepare myself is an erotic fantasy. I've been living on carrot sticks, cheese cubes, ham, and cracker biscuits. To make me a grilled cheese sandwich would be a grand romantic gesture.

When Paul is showered and rested, he tries to catch what light remains of the day and then attempts to sleep when we do. Sometimes he'll collapse on the bed and sleep for ten hours straight. Sometimes he'll pace the floor, unable to sleep, and so he turns to work.

The cycle continues for about a week, sleep, work, sleep, work. I resent that his employer gets the best of him, and home gets what remains. At least, while this goes on, he gets up to the children at night and I can bank some sleep. I've learned to accept this inbuilt delay before I get the time and attention, I feel is my due.

Before I know it Ruby is one-year-old. And I'm pregnant again.

6 PRECONCEPTIONS

September 2002

Lucy, a Birth Centre midwife, stops me in the hallway while I restock pamphlets.

'This is a bit unorthodox,' she says, 'and there's no obligation on your part, but would you be willing to visit a client of mine from a cultural minority? It's her first baby.'

She explains that the woman separated from her husband following an altercation. There's a Domestic Violence Order in place but limited support. A hospital social worker placed her in furnished accommodation, but Lucy knows she'll need more than an address to navigate the early weeks of mothering. Even as her midwife, Lucy doesn't have authority to visit her client at home.

'Would you be willing to visit? She just wants someone to talk to about pregnancy and birth. Her English is limited. And when the time comes, could you organise for FBC to take her some food? May I give her your number?'

It doesn't feel like a huge responsibility. Hanging out with pregnant women and newborn babies is exclusively all I've done since stepping into Friends of the Birth Centre. Morning teas for new mothers, the Parents and Babies Expo, I love doing it. When someone in the group has a baby, a meal for the freezer is the standard gift. I feel honoured that Lucy has asked.

'Of course. When do you want me to start?'

There's no compensation for food or petrol. I don't care. When we meet, she asks that I call her Rose, feeling her birth name would be unpronounceable. I don't speak her language or know her culture. I'm so painfully white and middle class. I do my best to listen. She takes comfort in the fact that I'm Catholic so I can't bring myself to tell her my care factor for religion these days falls in the range of zero. With no family or suitable friends, Rose asks me to go with her when labour begins. She seems so alone, I can hardly say no. It appears I'm to be her doula.

The home phone rings, and I answer it quickly on account of a sleeping baby. My best high school friend, and bridesmaid, Maria, has been living in Indonesia with her Australian partner.

The Bali Bombing was only months ago. Three explosions in a Kuta nightclub killed 202 young travellers, 88 of them Australian. As a result, our government has gifted all expatriate Australians a ticket home to reunite with their families.

'Everything's fine,' she reassures me. 'I just want to see you.'

Insecurity leaks like moisture from the sponge of our friendship. A lot has happened in three years. I've multiplied myself by two. She won't know I'm pregnant again.

I drive up the coast early to beat the traffic and knock on her parent's front door.

Maria opens it and, whoosh, the time warp of our friendship transports us straight back to the intimacy we shared as teenagers, crushing on boys and learning to drive. I meet her two-year-old son and we talk the afternoon away over multiple cups of tea.

I look at the clock, 'Gosh, Maria, I have to go.'

'What? No!' She puts her hand on my arm, as if to stop me. 'I thought we could go out tonight.'

'I need to be in Brisbane.'

I explain to her about Rose from the Birth Centre who's due to give birth any day.

'What's the chance she'll go into labour tonight?' Maria always had a strong influence on me.

'You're only one and a half hours away.'

I delivered ten frozen meals to Rose two days ago, carefully wrapped in foil for reheating in the oven, since she doesn't have a microwave. I'd enquired how she was feeling. She'd said she felt fine, no change. Maybe I can take a chance and have a night out with my friend?

'What do you think of Berardo's Restaurant?' I say.

'Divine,' Maria swoons.

She calls and makes a reservation in a business-like voice and then squeals that we got the last table. We hop in my car as thunder rumbles in the distance. There's bound to be a storm tonight.

We luck a carpark only one block away, a miracle on Hastings Street in the middle of the holidays. As we get out of the car my phone rings. I recognise the number.

'Rose? How are you?' Even face to face, our conversations are a challenge. Without the context of her body language, communicating on the phone will be difficult.

She says, 'I think...leaking,' and I try to determine whether she's experiencing a slow leak like I had with Elijah or whether her waters broke in a gush and we should expect something to happen soon.

'Have you had any pains?' I choose words that are easy to understand.

'No, I am good.'

It's her first baby. There's sure to be no rush. I can still enjoy dinner with Maria and then drive home to Brisbane. I tell her to call her midwife and to eat and drink and sleep now while she's comfortable. If anything changes, she can call me.

Maria and I are seated at our table by the kitchen with the aroma of garlic and seafood. The restaurant is full, bustling with staff, and the sound of pots and pans, clinking glasses, and clashing cutlery on plates. I put my phone on top of my handbag where I imagine I'll hear it. I get caught up, laughing, and talking. Only once dessert arrives do I remember to check my phone. I have three missed calls, twenty minutes apart. Thunder cracks and rolls above our heads.

We pay the bill and exit to the street where the rain is pounding down. There's nowhere quiet where I can listen to my voicemail, so we dash through the deluge to my car.

The first message: Rose explains she's having contractions but happy to stay home.

The second one is hard to understand but it sounds like she's in active labour. She asks me to come now.

The third one she puffs that she's calling a taxi and going to the Birth Centre. Can I please meet her there?

I feel sick. What was I thinking, being here? We buckle up and I realise I'm no longer one and a half hours from Brisbane. We didn't anticipate the return drive to Maria's house. Rose isn't answering her phone. She's probably at the Birth Centre now, and far too busy for phone calls anyway. The phone in the midwives' station rings off the hook. I leave a message asking for a call back regarding Rose's status.

Maria and I drive in deafening silence through the dark of the tropical storm. The wipers beat on high, causing glare from the headlights, and I still can't see the road. It takes our two pairs of eyes to navigate the drive. Traffic is crawling. Some cars pull over to wait it out.

'Breathe,' Maria reminds me. 'What's done is done.'

I call the Birth Centre a few more times and leave the same hopeless message. I'd like someone to tell me, one way or another, whether to make the risky drive to Brisbane tonight, or whether I've missed Rose's birth.

I deliver Maria to her gate. The downpour is easing slightly. We exchange a clammy hug, the console between the front seats presses my belly in a tender spot. Given the weather, she insists I stay in the car. I drive home at the pace of a snail, and as I hit the outskirts of Brisbane, I receive a call from Lucy's colleague, Ellen.

'Rose has both of us here and she's making great progress. The baby will be born soon. Don't come. Get some sleep. Come visit in the morning.'

The next day I buy the nicest bunch of flowers I can afford from the expensive florist inside the hospital. I want Rose to feel special, but really, it's an apology. When I see her, she looks tired but triumphant. She proudly presents her baby, Faith, and of course I want a cuddle. Evidently, my presence wasn't required. Rose was having her baby with two of the best midwives in the business.

7 DOULA

Mid-January 2003

Indigestion from the rich dinner with Maria has transmuted into the usual all day, all night, morning-sick exhaustion that I now take as a sign that all is well in my first trimester.

I accidentally let Rose slip down my priority list. It's been two weeks since I drove her and baby Faith home from the hospital, discovering in the process that she had already eaten all the frozen dinners I'd provided.

Since then, I've been busy heaving into the toilet, random garden beds, and once even stopped the car to vomit by the roadside. Today though, I pay her a visit with more frozen meals.

She opens the door looking fresh and rested. She has put some effort into appearances. I step inside her tidy kitchen where there are rows of glistening baby bottles on the drainer and a can of formula on the bench.

'You're not breastfeeding?'

'No, my milk, no good.'

'Of course, your milk is good!'

'Faith not stop crying in the night. She cry and cry. She not drink my milk. I not want,' she gestures to the next-door duplex, 'people to listen. Faith likes this milk. She sleep now.'

If I had visited her more in the early days would Rose have so readily switched to formula? The child health nurse will have visited. Maybe a social worker too. I wonder what support was given. Rose has a limited income and breast milk is free. At around $30 a week, by the time Faith turns one, this decision might cost Rose over a thousand dollars. That's a ticket home to her family. Can she afford to feed herself and her baby too?

'Where did you get the bottles?'

'My friend bought them. From church.'

I don't want to say anything that might upset her. Hospitals measure successful postnatal care, among other factors, by how many babies are still breastfeeding after three months. I'm glad she has support from folk in her church. I can see she loves her baby. All will be fine. She doesn't need me intruding on her life and her decisions.

I give Rose a tiny gift from my children, a plush giraffe on a plastic clip, and leave with a sense of having failed her twice. Later, I tell her midwife, Lucy, what happened.

'You can't make a woman breastfeed if she doesn't want to,' she assures me. 'We all have our cultural biases. Bottle feeding is her normal. You did your best!'

But I know that I didn't.

I log into my new favourite online forum, *Natural Parenting*. An old FBC member, Susan Stark, has started a grass roots magazine, and the forum is a bonus.

I'm member #12 – a keen early adopter. Participants get to know each other over topics like 'what does your toddler actually eat?' and 'is my baby feeding too frequently?' or 'is my baby getting enough sleep. Am I?'

We discuss books like *The Womanly Art of Breastfeeding* and *Fresh Milk, The Story of Breasts* and *The Continuum Concept*. Regarding pregnancy and birth, we refer to *The Thinking Woman's Guide to a Better Birth* and *Pursuing the Birth Machine*.

Topics that unite us are easily navigated. Everyone, including fathers on the forum, promote breastmilk as baby's first food, and feeding beyond the first year. We all agree about babywearing, basically keeping baby close and reject sleep training to instead endure the highs and lows of co-sleeping or play musical beds according to the family push and pull. We collectively wonder how to find a like-minded babysitter, and when necessary, navigate the social judgment of our parenting attitudes and practices.

We bond over cloth nappies and baby slings. We share tips on how to feed our babies discreetly in public, and regularly question whether we should have to be discreet at all? Intimate alliances are formed via threads dedicated to *Trying To Conceive*, *Recovering After Miscarriage*, and *Counting Down To Due Dates*. I feel genuine affection for people I've never actually met. We share our deepest secrets and call this virtual space our home.

These are people I can learn from. Thinking people, who scratch beneath the surface, ask hard questions, and do their own research. If I'm searching for evidence to support my choice – to use cough syrup (or not), ibuprofen (or not) – there are people only too willing to present some evidence and explain what they would do. Of course, caution prevails when taking advice from strangers, but these people are becoming less and less like strangers and more like neighbours, family, even.

If I'm not careful, I can waste hours at the computer. The forum is a great source of comfort and at the same time, a guilty pleasure. I'd be uncomfortable telling Paul exactly how many hours I'm spending online every day.

The draw for the Birth Centre is conducted once a month. The greatly anticipated call from Tamara finally comes. She doesn't mess about with pleasantries.

'Jodie, I have some news.' Her tone makes me uneasy, not her usual peppy style.

'I think I know what you're gonna say.'

'I'm so sorry. You were the third last name in the draw.'

'What does that mean?'

'It means, even allowing for the attrition rate, you won't get into the Birth Centre.'

'Oh…' My mind does circuits. What kind of arrogance was it that led me to think I could win the ballot three times in a row? I don't have a Plan B. I've given no thought to what I might do if I can't have Tamara for my midwife. I mean, of course I can have this baby on the ward. This is not my first rodeo. I'm an experienced mother now. I'll just have to make the best of this situation.

8 ACTIVIST

February 2003

In the year since I became convenor, Friends of the Birth Centre is going strong and morale is high. We had an idea to organise a public event but learned that new legislation since the events of 9/11 obliges us to obtain public liability insurance. So we shelved the idea until the funds were raised.

Our fearless prior-president Rebecca has announced she's expecting twins and unable to continue in her fundraising role due to debilitating nausea. Luck is with us. The new team is creative and energetic. They pick up and carry on. Our baby t-shirts continue to be hot merchandise, though not as profitable as we'd like. The hospital auspices the bake sale, featuring a raffle too, which raises several hundred dollars every other month. But it takes a small army of people to keep the money coming in, so we're still seeking a low input alternative that doesn't demand so much effort.

Our committee meets for dinner at a small restaurant in Chermside to plan our Annual General Meeting. We've tried to make it a child-free event, but nurslings are inseparable from mama so there are always a few babies. Apart from the clutter of prams and strollers, they're rarely a disruption.

Long-standing member, Hannah, looks around. 'How many of you are pregnant right now?'

We count ourselves off, amazed that seven of the twelve are pregnant and due within months of each other.

'And who got in? Have they drawn the ballot yet?'

The women break the news to each other. Five out of seven won the ballot to access the Birth Centre. Twins will exclude Rebecca but her midwife-mentor, Karen Marshall, co-founder of the Birth Centre, will attend her on the ward.

All faces turn to me.

'What about you, Jodie?'

I hesitate. 'I didn't get in.'

'But you'll get in later, right,' says Hannah, 'down the track?' Not every successful candidate will give birth at the Birth Centre. It's policy to refer out to specialists if complications arise.

'I was too far down the list for that.'

Around the table, a rising tone of disbelief, 'What? No!'

'It's going to be okay.' I'm unsure if I should reveal our arrangement, but all eyes are fixed with expectation. 'Tamara will squeeze me into her caseload.'

I know how lucky I am to have a relationship with my midwife that's personal enough that she'll stretch to give me the birth I want. Tamara won't make any money for the extra time. I wouldn't be consuming any more hospital resources than if I was birthing on the ward. It's technically against the rules, access being so restricted these days, but there's a collective sigh of relief around the table. I feel understood. I couldn't imagine having anyone else in the room while giving birth. Tamara knows my husband; he knows her. She knows our children and still celebrates their birthdays.

The ballot is a problem. The fourth room in the new Birth Centre increased capacity from around 30 women to 40 per month. Few people even know about it, but still the service is oversubscribed. Nowhere in this city but the Birth Centre offers midwife-led continuity of care. They achieve excellent outcomes. The caesarean rate is lower and breastfeeding rates are higher and women are overwhelmingly satisfied. Which begs the obvious question: Why don't more hospitals have Birth Centres?

We revisit our ambition to stage an event. We have a point to make.

'We could string prayer flags around the hospital with names of all the women who've missed the ballot that month,' our secretary, Emma, suggests.

'We could shape the flags like baby onesies,' says Hannah.

Ripples of 'oooh!' circle the table.

'Or make it a washing line with baby clothes.'

'We'd be airing their dirty laundry!'

We laugh at our chutzpah. I'm loving everyone's passion laid bare at the table.

Emma suggests, 'We could find a neutral location.'

I add, 'With lots of people in the daytime.'

Emma works in marketing. I see where she's going. There's no need for marching and chanting. But with a bit of media attention, maybe the hospital will take notice.

'I love it,' says Emma. 'It feels right.'

I have tingles. I think everyone else does too.

We decide that International Day of the Midwife, this year coinciding with Labour Day, is the only appropriate day. There are clichés here for journalists to exploit: babies, midwives, labour. It's also the week before Mother's Day. Maybe we can stretch public interest to the following week?

The evening passes in ecstatic conversation. There's much work to do before May. We all go home high on shared energy.

February 2003

For Elijah's third birthday I've outdone myself with a pirate theme. It took two days to make his cake: a treasure chest from a Women's Weekly cookbook with strings of liquorice, chocolate gold coins, and sugar pearls spilling out from under the chocolate lid.

My friend Kareena is here with baby Noah, born at Selangor Private Hospital on the Sunshine Coast. None of the Brisbane hospitals could offer continuity of care with a midwife for a vaginal birth after caesarean, written VBAC, and pronounced vee-back, which is essentially just a normal vaginal birth. At Selangor, midwives work caseload. Some had their own practices before insurance collapsed and crushed their businesses.

Our babysitter is also here to celebrate, along with my mothers' group friends. Special guests are Paul's sister, Kay, her husband, Andrew, and their two school-age children, who recently moved to Brisbane. I've enjoyed having family close by. But something's not right about Andrew's skin tone today. He's an awful shade of yellow, which his daring orange shirt does little to camouflage. I can see he's doing his best to be a friendly guest and a doting uncle, but I notice the set of Kay's jaw, and the furrow between her brows. It doesn't feel right to ask about it, in the noise and mayhem of a children's birthday party, so I let it go.

The Annual General Meeting is better attended than ever before, and suddenly we have a half dozen new members keen to engage with FBC. Time being of the essence, we lock in the plan. We'll erect ten iconic rotary clotheslines in a public place, loaded with baby clothes to symbolise unmet demand for midwifery services in our region. All other maternity organisations are welcome to participate.

Core planners, Emma, Kath and I, share our plan with Marg Fien and Karen Marshall, founders of the Birth Centre. They pull out the ballot records and collectively estimate the number of women who missed the ballot. It turns out to be such a round number we have to recalculate it. Four thousand women and 4000 babies in the past five years. We clutch this information and run with it. Acquiring exactly 4000 items of baby clothes will be our goal. I post it to the community on *Ozmidwifery* and my local *Natural Parenting* sub-group. We enlist support from Brisbane Birth Action Group and the Home Midwifery Association of Queensland and put an appeal in the newsletter to all the past members of FBC – a substantial number of people – seeking donations of baby clothes to help us reach our goal.

As a courtesy, we schedule a meeting with Public Relations at the Royal to explain our intention to protest. The junior marketing representative smiles at our naivety and wishes us luck. It's apparent that PR would never let us demonstrate on the hospital campus. The Midwifery Unit Manager, who's regularly accused of being a gatekeeper between the progressive Birth Centre and the more conservative Birth Suites, is also in attendance. She waits for the marketing person to leave, then grins and shakes our hands.

'Good on you ladies! We can't help you with your event, but perhaps you don't know that King George Square is available for community events?'

'In front of City Hall? It sounds expensive.' I nervously eyeball Emma and Kath. We're full of bluster. FBC doesn't have money for that.

'No harm in enquiring,' she winks.

We do enquire and discover that, for community groups and events such as ours, the permit's absolutely free!

April 2003

My belly is definitely on show now. Today is play group, hosted by Becky. We met via the *Natural Parenting* forum. She delights the children with her sweet songs and games. They especially love the magical stories she creates with a tableau of coloured silks, wooden blocks, natural rocks and tiny people handmade from sticks and felted tufts of wool.

Becky has brought a friend along who's a photography student. She asks if Gemma-Rose can take some photos of the children. We discuss my pregnancy and the Birth Centre.

Gemma-Rose asks, 'Are you inclined to take birth photos?'

I tell her some people think it's weird, but not me. 'The midwives are usually available to take a happy snap or two.'

'I'd love to photograph a birth,' Gemma-Rose says wistfully. 'I've taken pregnancy photos. And newborn photos for my sister, but not a birth.'

'Well, I'm happy to call you if I go into labour at a realistic hour of the day.'

'That would be amazing!'

And, just like that, I've invited a stranger to my baby's birth.

I'll have to somehow explain this to Paul.

9 MEDIA TART

April 2003

My belly expands as the deadline for Airing Our Laundry approaches. Since Labour Day is a public holiday, there's an unexpected fee of $200 for clean-up of King George Square after our event. Friends of the Birth Centre don't have the funds to spare, so I pay it out of pocket for peace of mind. We're committed, with no contingency plan.

I'm stressed to my eyeballs. I don't know how to delegate because I don't know what needs to be done until I encounter it, and so I handle it. The women in FBC are working around my improvisational style with aplomb, never complaining about the mess in my wake. We've been meeting fortnightly and, with less than three weeks to go, nerves are becoming frayed. From my desk, I can see through the front door to where Hannah is parking her red Morris Mini. She's early and I'm not ready.

'Did a cyclone blow through or something?' she takes in the state of the house with last night's dishes in the sink. Kiddie clutter swamps the floor.

'Sorry, that's dinner and breakfast. I meant to get to it, but the printer is jammed.' The paperless office isn't happening here and in thirty minutes there'll be nine or ten people, plus their little ones, squeezing into my living room. My desk is a chaos of sticky notes and crumpled paper from the printer. What's the point of writing an agenda if I can't print it out?

Hannah picks up the dishcloth, 'You fix it, I'll clean up.'

Kath, the stalls coordinator, is next to arrive. They tackle the kitchen sink and the basket of laundry on the couch while I finish printing the agenda and figuring out how to delegate.

Dani arrives next. Her belly is as big as mine. She brings three small children, Iced Vo Vos, and a wicker laundry basket full of pegs she bought at the dollar store. Already we have seven children to entertain, and fewer than half of us are here.

'Wait Kathy, where's that basket?' I realise she's washing my shrivelled-but-clean, unfolded laundry.

'What did I do?'

'Never mind,' I fumble, 'You've done a wonderful thing. What would I do without you girls?'

I log into the *Natural Parenting* forum and announce Airing Our Laundry in the *Events* section. I post it to *Ozmidwifery* too, and several midwives call to tell me how their local Birth Centres, in Townsville, Gladstone and Bundaberg, were closed in the last ten years due to budget cuts. The threat of closure hangs over small services, like Mareeba and Mossman, in North Queensland, 'centralising' their services in other districts, where the efficiency of active management – induced labour accompanied by an epidural – takes priority over the woman's experience. The downside, that women get more stitches, episiotomies, forceps, ventouse, and caesarean deliveries, seems lost on the number crunchers. Long term reproductive and genital health isn't really on their radar. Emails pour through my workstation, story upon story of women feeling stripped of their rights in childbirth and supporting our intention to protest.

I take breaks to feed children, surf forum, do housework, email, feed children, make and answer as many phone calls as I can while they sleep, email, feed children, feed self, put kids to bed, email, surf forum, and sleep. Sometimes Paul complains that he never sees me anymore. Sometimes we sit in companionable silence, working on our respective computers well into the night.

I receive a message from a woman called Caroline McCullough offering to help develop a marketing plan to maximise our impact and draw people to our event. She apologises that she can't help more because she's due any day with her second baby.

When we meet in her home, Caroline's belly looks ready to burst. Our conversation, like any two pregnant women meeting for the first time, goes like this:

I ask, 'Where are you having your baby?' She already knows I'm at the Birth Centre.

'This one will be born at the Mater Mothers.'

'Is that where Benjamin was born?'

'No, The Wesley. He turned three last February.'

'Really? Elijah's a February baby too.'

Caroline asks, 'What day?'

'The sixteenth.'

'No way!'

What are the odds we should meet in this way, our first babies born on the same day?

I gesture towards Elijah. 'He was born around one in the morning.'

She half-smiles. 'Benjamin was born in work hours. It was a scheduled induction.'

She tells me about his birth. How the induction didn't take, and the cascade of interventions meant Benjamin was born by caesarean due to 'failure to progress' and how the epidural immobilised her but didn't make her numb. How she could feel the entire surgery. How the doctors discussed the football over her, naked and frozen, like she wasn't even there. How the anaesthetist gave her a general the instant he realised she was becoming distressed. How she woke up scared, alone and confused, with no baby. Caroline says her new obstetrician, incidentally, a woman, is pressuring her to schedule a caesarean. She'll lose her opportunity for a vaginal birth unless she goes into labour naturally. And soon. The countdown has started.

'Caroline, do you remember, there was a flood somewhere in the African delta, about two weeks after our boys were born? The water was rising, and a pregnant woman and her family were rescued from the treetops above their home.'

Caroline's eyes grow wide. 'I remember that!'

In the time it took to scramble to safety, the woman had given birth in a tree. By nature's amazing design, her adrenaline state helped her eject her baby as a survival reflex. They would both have been lost if the floodwaters had swept the mother away, but she was strong enough to hold on, both to the tree and her baby, and the pair were airlifted out just in time.

Caroline admits, 'I cried for days, every time I thought about it.'

'Me too,' I relent. We both grow teary together, remembering the impact of that story in our fragile postnatal states. Nothing really prepares you for the intensity of those feelings. Nothing has dulled them either, though maybe with time. My mother claims it did for her.

Caroline sits a little taller, pushes her chin a little higher. 'My body knows what to do,' she says.

'You know it does,' I say. The media coaching session begins. We don't know it yet, but Caroline and I will make memories together.

More emails, more errands. The only real record of what's going on is inside my head, purged into occasional email reports I send to the committee to keep them up to date. I have a lot on my plate, two kids and one on the way, a relationship with my regularly absent husband, and a plethora of involvements, both online and in real life, including a promise I now regret, to organise my high school reunion. All feed my creative energy but deplete my domestic energy. One night, after a small conflict with Paul over the state of the kitchen, I storm off to the bedroom for a good, hard, cry.

There were many tears in my first two pregnancies. This time, I've felt exceptionally level. But now I'm hiding in the bedroom, snivelling into a too-wet tissue, feeling sorry for myself. Paul comes and sits with me. I talk at him about the number of jobs I haven't done, how many phone calls I have to make, how the kids have play group tomorrow but I don't have the time, and I'm behind on the washing anyway, so what are they going to wear? How it's impossible to finish anything I start due to constant interruptions, but they're our children, so how can I resent them? I've no idea what to make for dinner. I'm overwhelmed. And why am I so itchy?

Paul holds me until the stream subsides.

'Remember, I'm here. You're not doing everything alone. I want to help.'

I wipe my nose on his shoulder. He doesn't pull away.

'Are you hungry?' he offers. I shake my head.

'I'll feed the kids. You rest. We'll have something light to eat later, okay?'

Over eggs on toast that night, Paul tells me we're getting a cleaner and there's nothing more to say on the matter. I agree to put pride in my pocket and give it a trial run.

10 AIRING OUR LAUNDRY

May 2003

Armed with Caroline's marketing advice, I realise we haven't promoted the event heavily enough. I'm an amateur with none of the tools of an experienced event promoter. I worry that we failed to contact the politicians that Brisbane Birth Action Group's self-appointed agitator, Bruce Teakle, advised we approach. I worry that we'll embarrass ourselves. For Pete's sake, we have a child singing and dancing to a recording for crowd entertainment. Did I mention there's no stage?

I receive a call from a journalist wanting to know more about our event. Hooray! She listens politely and is able to recount the important details. She wants a photograph to go with her story for the Sunday paper. Yippee! I run through a mental list of suitable subjects and rest upon Ali, my yoga buddy, and her two-month-old baby Jackson. Ali missed out on the ballot. And she has a Hills Hoist in her garden. I ask, and she obliges.

It'll be a morning shoot on Saturday. Around 8 am would be ideal, when babies are brightest. The journalist says they can't make it before 10 am. Every mother knows that a small baby is likely to sleep then, but we have to take that chance.

Saturday comes and I nervously drag a bag of props, nappies and onesies, to Ali's house. She's thinking the same thing and has already pegged a bunch of tie-dyed baby clothes on her clothesline. All of us in FBC had agreed to keep all hippy-dippy references at arm's length. We want to be perceived as mainstream. But the photographer loves the tie-dye, so that's what he gets. He takes a bunch of photos, then suggests we peg baby Jack to the clothesline.

Ali and I make brief eye contact. She looks unsure but agrees to give it a go. I step in to help her button Jack's little bib and brace over the wire for safety. The photographer is ready and with a one, two, three, Ali gently lets him dangle.

Jack disappears inside his denim overalls. His little legs kick, his arms flail, his face is hidden but for eyes peering over the bib. The crotch studs could pop any second. Ali's hands hover underneath, obviously in shot. The photographer's camera clickety clicks, but I think we all know those images will be useless.

He apologises for the suggestion and all agree that Ali should just hold Jack pegged to the line. He gets the shot and, subsequently, leaves for his next job. The whole experience leaves me doubting whether it has been worthwhile. Did we get a picture good enough for the papers? Will Ali still like me after this? I feel like I'm exploiting people and abusing all my friendships.

That night, I plan ahead and pack the car. I tick off my check sheet, but I still feel there's something I've forgotten. My head is so busy with details that I hardly sleep. Adrenaline is causing the baby to kick much more than usual. I've never loved that Paul travels, but I'm glad he isn't here tonight for me to disturb his sleep. He'll be boarding a flight home from Beijing shortly, and I'll meet him with the children in the early morning at King George Square. The forecast, thankfully, is for good weather.

I get up for a glass of milk at 3 am and compulsively check my email. Suddenly it comes to me: I haven't done the laundry. I have nothing to wear! I consider whether I have time to wash and dry my best maternity shirt. I decide it's more important to get some rest.

At 6 am I pack the kids into their car seats with the many bags of donated baby clothes stacked to the roof around them. We leave the house with breakfast dishes on the table. There's no time to buy a newspaper. Picture in the paper or not, we must still go through the motions of today. At the traffic lights, I smudge my face with lipstick in the rear-view mirror.

Part of me is quaking to see the whole display en masse. Until today, it has just been an idea. I drive around the corner and see that people are gathering for set up. As soon as Hannah arrives with the trailer of clotheslines everyone knows the drill and the blokes, husbands and brothers and fathers, get it underway like clockwork. I have to stop for a second and breathe, allow myself to take it all in.

Never let it be said that burly men don't get women's business. At FBC events I've met men from all walks of life, with tears in their eyes, telling me about their experiences with wives and partners and daughters in the Birth Centre. I've heard men defying the formula advocates to help their partners breastfeed. They know what women need as well as anyone else.

The guys position the clothesline bases, 40 kilograms apiece, in their designated triangle on the pavement. Helpers emerge from the gathering crowd to hang the clothes and before we know it, the installation is complete. We turn the cranks, raising them high, and step back to admire the spectacle.

I make a dozen new friends. Many of them wield the heavy Sunday newspaper. Page two, with a ludicrous full-colour photograph of my friend with her baby pegged to her clothesline. No labour or pushing clichés to be found.

It reads: *"Mums peg hope on new line of protest"*

There aren't many people in King George Square on the Sunday of a long weekend, but the hundred or so who've come are here thanks to *The Sunday Mail.*

People are craning their necks to see all the cute baby clothes. They strain to read the cloth nappies we embroidered with Birth Centre ballot history. It looks amateur, with our trestle tables making a rectangle around the end of the display. I wish it were more polished. But we achieved our goal. It's of curiosity to passers-by. They ask us about it. We tell them. They didn't know it was important before today. Now they do.

The Birth Centre midwives are here to support us. I never expected them to come, but their presence is a loving show of support.

The six of us who are pregnant in the FBC committee line up in front of City Hall for a photo. We turn our bodies sideways for effect. The Belly Brigade. Someone brings the vocal PA forward, and a child sings a sweet song, captivating the young parents. Then we offer the microphone to anyone who wants to speak. Thankfully, a few people step up and tell their stories.

I drift from group to group in a whirl of discussion with an assortment of people for most of the day. Many of them I've corresponded with by email. It's wonderful to finally meet them in person.

Some of these people have been activists for many years and generously offered their advice for this event. Bruce Teakle is here, from Brisbane Birth Action Group. He's a tall man with a kind face, a gap-toothed smile and a country air. He introduces me to GP/Obstetrician, Dr Sarah Buckley, author of *Ecstatic Birth*, and she softly shakes my hand. I'm awestruck, having read her numerous articles on the internet, including the story of her youngest daughter's unattended birth. She's much smaller and quieter than her bold articles about unhindered childbirth would have you think.

Media arrives and they want an interview. With me? This is beyond our expectations and I didn't prepare for television. Caroline's advice was to speak in short sentences, use concise language, stick to the topic, have stock answers ready for anticipated questions.

There are two cameras on me. They're chasing a snappy sound bite for the evening news. I glance down at my protruding belly that accentuates the pilling on my much loved, third time around, stretchy black, second-best, maternity shirt. In my head, I curse the vision of a better outfit at the bottom of my laundry pile.

The reporter repeats a question that he's already asked off-camera. My mind goes blank.

I ramble on and on about Birth Centres, what they are, what makes them safe, and what midwives do, about the ballot at the Birth Centre highlighting how many more women would choose it if they could. It feels good to blurt it all out, and my nervous ramble continues until I must stop for breath.

The interview is over. The journalist thanks me as the camera operator packs everything up. My agonised soliloquy broke the 'short sentences, three-second grab' rule. What an amateur!

Around 2 pm we break down the display. Spirits are high among The Belly Brigade, but I feel deflated and fatigued. I may have blown it. Paul arrived earlier from his flight. We drive away in silence; the children crashed out in their car seats, and we don't even unpack the car when we get home.

We made mistakes. People asked us why was Right To Life permitted to have a stall? They didn't sign up using that name. A stage and a spokesperson would have had more impact. We could have had panel discussions, and much more entertainment. Several people pointed out that I'd missed an opportunity to leverage the fact I'd missed the ballot. But we won't make those mistakes again. Suckers for punishment, Paul and I go straight inside to catch the six o'clock news.

Thank the universe for synergy and a slow news night. There we are in technicolour, on three commercial channels. One features my fumbled interview. We're the seventh story in, the feel-good segment before the sport. In the news grabs, the washing lines, plus all the bellies and babies, did the hard work for us. Scenes from our demonstration feature again in the highlights at 10 pm. I'm grateful to have managed a single, tightly edited, modestly sensible, two-second factual quote: the number of women per month on the waiting list. The team debrief via email and we all go to bed feeling different. The effort was worth it and we'd learned so much. We can do it again and do it better.

11 SHIRLEY VALENTINE

May 2003

Since our event, I've discovered the broader network of activists. I decide to attend Birth Action Group meetings as Friends of the Birth Centre's vested representative. My first meeting is at the glamorous Clayfield home of a midwife and childbirth educator. It seems too impossibly tidy for a place where children live. The group agree that Brisbane Birth Action Group should become the Queensland chapter of the national group, Maternity Coalition. A sociologist and author, Kereen Reiger, founded the association five years ago via the amalgamation of several like-minded maternity consumer groups in New South Wales and Victoria.

It's a major step for Queensland, but the significance of the moment is upstaged when Bruce ropes me into doing a segment on Channel Seven's current affairs show *Today Tonight* with himself and Dr Sarah Buckley. She's the hormones expert and homebirth advocate. He'll present the *National Maternity Action Plan* – the blueprint Medicare could follow to create universal primary midwifery care in Australia. I'm the token pregnant person. With no idea what I've agreed to, I bring in my friend Kareena, to tell her VBAC story too.

The segment will begin with a woman whose local hospital refused to attend her baby's frank breech, or bottom-first, birth.

The camera crew arrives at my door as Dr Buckley tackles the mess of dishes in my sink.

The journalist, Lexy Hamilton-Smith, asks Kareena and me about our birth choices. They film cutaways of the children and of my hand on my very large belly. They interview Bruce and Sarah in my courtyard while I keep the children quiet. They film another cutaway of Sarah pretend-working at my computer. The mouse isn't even plugged in. Lexy then completes her 'noddies', slightly ridiculous shots of her reacting to our answers, which will be edited in later. They leave, advising the segment will be televised in the next few weeks.

Late May 2003

Six weeks before I'm due to give birth, Paul's sister Kay, brings Andrew, her husband, home from palliative care. He's in the final stages of liver cancer. She seems so strong, holding the whole world together for their children. And so, I continue to juggle my not-nearly-so-heavy stuff. There's just the school reunion to get through and I'll be ready to have this baby.

It's dinnertime. The phone rings, and Paul answers. Andrew has fallen out of bed and Kay can't lift him. Can Paul come?

I feel such remorse for avoiding Andrew. If I saw him, skin and bone, jaundiced with distant, sunken eyes, it might crack my shell. I'm cooking meals for friends and strangers while my sister-in-law cares for everyone, alone. Where are my priorities?

Paul is gone only a minute or two and the phone rings again. I expect that he may have forgotten something, but it's my father's voice on the line. 'Hello, Jo.'

'Dad?' I'm sure I sound surprised. He calls so rarely.

'Listen,' he continues without a pause, 'your mother, she's gone.'

'Gone...shopping?'

I hear him sigh.

'Her wardrobe is empty. All her personal things are gone.'

It takes a few moments to compute. The baby lurches in my belly.

'No!'

Dad continues, unemotional, in shock, 'She left a note on the table. Do you want me to read it?'

I really, really don't. This is territory I never expected to traverse with my father. We've rarely shared deep conversations.

'Uh, okay.'

I listen to my father, in a puzzled kind of voice, read the Dear John letter from my mother. I turn over my memories from last weekend when I surprised them, turning up at their door after school reunion business. I figured I'd be in strife if I was in town and didn't call in.

'You've been decluttering, Mum,' I'd said.

'I'm simplifying,' she'd snapped.

'Good on you for letting stuff go!' It was condescending. I was never a fan of her collectibles. The house had looked fresh and light.

I remember how the phone rang several times, which Mum had rushed to answer. Unusually, she'd closed the door behind her. I hadn't thought anything of it.

The note makes me curl up inside. My mother announced she has left us all, including my brother, in the week of Dad's retirement, and me, six weeks before bringing a new grandchild into the family. The selfish part of my heart that's preparing for childbirth needs to block this out too. I cannot face the slow death of my brother-in-law or the sudden breakdown of my family.

I hang up the phone, turn my invisible shield of denial up a notch or two, and carry on getting ready for tomorrow's committee meeting. FBC is so large now, we've adopted the Grange Library as our home.

But you can't hold back a waterfall. That night, after Paul returns, I take the phone into the bedroom and call Mum's closest sister. She is, we all are, surprised that Mum would up and leave in that manner. I blubber when she admits she'd always doubted they were happy. I go to bed and weep for my degraded relationship with Mum. And for Dad, who didn't see it coming and probably should have.

The next day I'm puffy and numb and itchy. I call prior-president Bec, at bursting point with twins. I explain what has happened and apologise for bailing on the meeting. Can she chair for me? She's sympathetic and says all the right things. Like a classic midwife, she orders me to eat well and look after myself.

June 2003

'Where are we going today, Mum?'

The internet of things is a decade away. My responsibilities require actual forms, on actual paper, to be posted, or handed over a counter at a physical office. I drag the children along to play group, and Mothers' Morning Teas at the hospital, and additional FBC commitments that include debriefing the new members we've acquired thanks to our recent visibility. Many have wonderful skills and happily assist. Some of them, like Kareena and Caroline, are disqualified from the Birth Centre. They're our most passionate volunteers.

For expediency, I begin to time small errands for when I know the children need to nap. I pile us all in the car and drive until they sleep. The reality of waking them so I can buy a book of stamps, a bottle of milk, a loaf of bread or a tank of petrol, is too difficult to consider. Leaving them in the car is a small risk. A calculated risk. I feel guilty about dragging them from pillar to post almost every day of the week, but I also get a buzz out of getting things done. I feel accomplished. It's becoming a compulsion.

A friend has organised a sweet shipment of handmade baby shoes. I need to put money in her account to cover the cost of my order: cute little soft-soled moccasins, first shoes for this baby. It has slipped down my list of priorities and now become urgent.

I drive through the shopping centre car park and debate whether I can transfer the funds while the kids sleep in the car. My self-talk goes, *don't leave a single mum short of cash*. I could lug two sleeping children – one in a stroller and one on my shoulder, but then there's my ever-present belly. Who am I kidding? My kids aren't that portable. They're so deeply asleep in their car seats that I convince myself they're safe.

I scout for a shady park, deciding on the taxi rank outside the bank, though it's illegal to park there. I roll the windows down just enough for ventilation, and to prevent anyone from reaching inside to force entry. I won't be able to see the children from inside the bank, but they'll be just outside the glass window. My sleep-deprived logic convinces me the risk is worthwhile if I can get this inconsequential errand done. In my world, in this moment, it makes bizarre sense. I check the windows, lock the doors, and walk away.

The bank is crowded, and the queue is long. I fill out the deposit slip and join the end of the line, fingering my car keys and worrying whether a child might wake up in my absence. What if someone sees them abandoned and sleeping? Five minutes later the teller explains that my bank can't transfer directly to the other party's building society. I must withdraw the cash and go directly to the building society itself. I ask where it is and she says it's just around the corner'. I don't know this shopping mall, but I believe she means It's close, and maybe this task can still be achieved today.

Ten minutes have elapsed when I return to the car. The children are still sleeping deeply, and the cabin is cool. At this point I could abort my mission, unlock the car, get in, drive away, but I don't.

I re-enter the mall and speed-walk around the corner beyond my bank, expecting to find the building society right there, but it isn't. Further ahead is the customer information centre. X marks the spot. You Are Here. I run my finger down the index and find the building society on the map. It's two aisles away!

I think about giving up but I've come this far. I run to the building society like a lumbering elephant, holding my belly, even though it's the only part of me now that doesn't jiggle. There's a queue but it moves quickly, and I deposit the money, obtain my receipt and run back towards the car, limping in breathless as a beached whale. It's taken ten, maybe fifteen minutes, tops.

I burst out of the mall with car keys at the ready. I check the children – thankfully still sleeping – bounce into the car and start the engine. Immediately, a police car arrives, blocking my exit. Two male officers get out and talk with a frowny parking attendant whose head doesn't move, but her eyes glare at me. Did she just nod with satisfaction?

I suddenly see myself on *Candid Camera*. Or *Cops*.

The constables are kind but firm. They tell me to turn off the engine and step out of the car for questioning. Humiliation heats my face and I know anxious red blotches flush my chest and neck. I apologise profusely and explain my situation. What kind of risk was I taking? What sickos might see my children and scare them, or hurt them? I read in the news that a sleeping child in Portugal was recently abducted from a hotel room while her parents ate in the restaurant downstairs. And here are my own children in full public view. I believed that would work to protect them. I must be out of my mind. The policemen observe my large belly; the children sleeping.

'Ma'am,' they say with kindness, 'we can see your predicament, but this is not a legal place to park. It's also illegal to leave your children in the car. We're not going to charge you but consider this a warning.'

'Thank you, officers!'

Shame sinks like lead in the pit of my stomach. I'm dressed for town, with make-up and jewellery. What if I'd worn my tracksuit, or pyjamas? What if my skin was not white and my car not a late model Toyota? Would they have been so kind?
I should have known better. Done better.

At home, I can't even begin to explain it to Paul. It would start a fight. I log in to the forum and purge into a confessional post. I need to tell someone. Fortunately, our play group friend Becky is online.

'No harm done,' she writes. *'Lesson learned. You're NOT a bad mother.'*

I calm down. Then I go back and delete the post before anyone else can see it.

12 LIFE ONLINE

June 2003

On Monday, I waddle up Kareena's steep driveway with Ruby in my arms. My belly sticks out so far that my thighs bump the underside as I climb. Elijah is at day-care because it's yet another errand day. The television is unfortunately always on, but there's a sandpit in the back yard where Elijah likes to play.

I knock on Kareena's front door, then open it and let myself in. She's already pouring a glass of water and offering me a chair in her living room. Baby Noah lies in a bassinet beside her chair. Kareena knows about Mum.

She hands me the glass, 'Gosh Jodie, how are you feeling?'

'I really don't know. I can't make sense of it. I don't want to think about it until the reunion is out of the way.'

'That came around fast,' she says, taking her chair.

'And Paul flew out yesterday, so it's just me and the kids. Dad will have to babysit. He's never had the children by himself.'

'Probably do him good, you know. A chance to connect with his grandchildren. What are you going to tell them?'

I shrug. 'They're bound to ask where Nana is.'

We sit for a moment and listen. Noah babbles. The mood lifts and I realise; this too shall pass.

I just have to get through the reunion. I'm embarrassed by the size of my belly, that I'll meet high school acquaintances from 16 years ago. What if someone asks about my folks? It's a small town. I don't want to intrude on Dad's privacy, but I'm not a convincing liar.

I bounce Ruby on my lap. She's getting cranky and we'll have to go soon. I lean her back in my arms to soothe her to sleep with my fingers running slowly through her soft, curly hair. I notice a minute dark spot on her scalp. I casually scratch it off with my fingernail and it moves.

'What's this? Can we turn the light on?'

I search through Ruby's hair, but I can't see anything else. I pick the crawling spot off with two fingers, pulling it down the shaft of her hair. She objects, but now I have it on my fingertip.

I hold it up to the light and my naked eye detects a distinctly insect-like shape.

'Kareena, what does this look like to you?'

I gag and apologise profusely to my friend. She finds my horror amusing.

With instructions to apply lavender oil and use a fine-toothed comb, our exit is deliberately swift.

I stop at the chemist and collect Elijah from day-care, itching all the way home. I slather Elijah and Ruby with hair conditioner and delouse them, primate style. They wriggle and complain, but the job gets done. I slather my own head with conditioner and lavender and a shudder slips out with every louse in the comb. No wonder I was itchy! How could I have let this happen? The reunion is mere days away. It's one more thing. Almost one too many.

The reunion goes smoothly. Everyone seems to have a good time. I forget to prepare clothes for myself (again), but I borrow Dad's tuxedo shirt and make do. My belly prompts the sharing of many stories.

Moana's first son was born by caesarean because the placenta attached itself over the cervix, blocking the baby's exit. Her second was also caesarean since the placenta, this time, grew into her prior uterine scar. Her second son was delivered safely, but she haemorrhaged to an extent the doctor performed a hysterectomy. There will be no more children for her, but she's grateful for her boys and that her life was spared.

Brett's ex-wife is a high-powered lawyer who scheduled surgery to maximise her maternity leave. She found the transition to motherhood difficult, but it never occurred to him to take time off from work and share the load. I'm unsurprised that they're no longer married. He only sees his child every second weekend.

Davina had twins, describing her labour as quick and painless. She managed to drive herself from home to hospital, but her husband was running late. She pushed out the first baby but waited until Dad arrived before birthing the second baby. Her story is one of those joyful-ridiculous tales you hear doing the rounds in my network; giving us hope that birth, even an unconventional one, can be normal and human and healthy.

I arrive home and find an email from Bec's husband, announcing that their twins, head down for the past month, were born safely with expert assistance from her mentor-midwife, Karen. It's the perfect outcome for what they considered a high-risk pregnancy. I reply with my congratulations and, after all the chaos I created for myself, I finally feel ready for my turn to come.

You gain strength, courage and confidence by every experience in which you really stop to look fear in the face...

Eleanor Roosevelt

WHAT DOES IT FEEL LIKE BEING BORN?

13 HOLDING THE SPACE

July 2003

It's Friday, and my due date.

Paul has tickets to the rugby semi-final at Suncorp Stadium. It's not my thing, but I'm happy for him to go.

'If anything happens, you'll call me straight away?' He pats the pocket of his jacket containing his phone.

I kiss him goodbye, feeling certain that nothing will happen.

A few hours later I feel crampy. After putting the children to bed, I time the contractions. They're irregular but seem to be fifteen minutes apart. Nothing to panic about. I get up to make tea and grip the door jamb to let the discomfort pass. In the kitchen, another one comes. I lean into the bench and breathe.

My previous births took a whole day to escalate. From active labour to pushing was around five hours. I don't have to worry about accidentally having a baby at home, do I?

I remember my forum-now-real-life friend, Kate, not believing she was in active labour. She gave birth on the toilet to the sound of sirens on her street.

I call Paul and tell him what's going on.

'I'm not saying to come home. Just that I'm having contractions and don't know what they mean.'

The game has only just started. We both know that at the game's end it can take an hour to exit the stadium with the crowd, walk to the car and navigate the detours to home.

'You know what they say about third babies. I can hardly watch the game here while you're pacing the floor. Put the telly on. I'm coming home.'

I need to visit the toilet and this time I feel enormous relief. By the time Paul parks in the garage, my contractions have notably subsided.

'All that for a poo?'

I blush, grateful he'd rather be here with me than at the game. Or at least, that he can pretend he would.

The next morning, Saturday, at the committee meeting, I joke with the girls about bringing my baby to the New Mothers' Morning Tea on Monday.

Sunday morning, contractions begin again, weak, but uncomfortable enough to distract me all day. In the evening, I put on a load of washing and go to bed early, anticipating a busy Monday, and it's a good thing I do.

Around 3.30 am, I wake up to a bright full moon, feeling irritable and hot, with contractions regular and mildly painful. Since I can't sleep, I get up and hang out the washing.

Afterwards, I attempt more sleep but manage only minutes here and there as contractions become more real and uncomfortable. Our dear kitty cat turns up to comfort me, purring against my belly.

At 6 am, I can't wait any longer. I call Tamara to tell her we're having a baby. I call our sitter too, who is to mind the children, since I still haven't heard from my mother. Thankfully, it's daylight now and our support groups can assist. In the car, I remember Gemma-Rose, the photographer, and send her an SMS saying that if she turns up at the Birth Centre around 9 am there should be plenty of time to take photos.

Paul and I arrive at 8 am. I greet Tamara with a long thank-you hug. She already has the tub filled, knowing my preference for water. If she's tired from having four clients this month, she doesn't show it. I thank her again for taking me on. 'Jodie,' she says, 'how could I let anyone else be your midwife?' After an excruciating, but compulsory, 20 minutes strapped to the foetal heart monitor, I'm upright and pacing the room until I feel ready to get in the tub. There's a timid knock at the door as Gemma-Rose arrives with a suitcase of camera equipment. She asks me politely what she can and can't do. I suggest she take all the photos she likes so long as she's out of my line of sight. With boundaries set, I withdraw to a trance and breathe through the growing discomfort. I've no concept of time, but I already know I'm not going to replicate Ruby's dynamic birth.

No one coaches. No one even speaks. I didn't bother to select any music. The silence feels right. Tamara periodically checks the baby's heart tones with a Doppler. When she sees I'm flagging, she puts a mirror on the bottom of the bath so I can observe some tiny glimmer of progress. It's encouraging, but I need things to happen slowly. When Tamara calls in the second midwife, I know she thinks I'm getting close.

Soon I begin pushing, and it's really hard work. After what seems like hours, but is probably just one, the splitting pain and my spontaneous growl tells me that the head is right there. One more push and that familiar 'pop'. Tamara reaches down and explains to me she's unlooping the cord from his neck. No drama. Paul and I remain calm. Follow on contractions are a long time coming and I feel the baby wriggle. I think about changing position but, with half a baby hanging out of me underwater, movement feels precarious.

A few pushes later, he's born – but very flat and blue. Tamara advises Paul and I to massage him for a few moments, with little response. Tamara then cuts the cord and begins rubbing him roughly and together the midwives perform resuscitation with a teeny mask attached via a hand pump to an oxygen canister. He's making a gurgling noise, like there's air moving through fluid in his throat. It gives me confidence. He'll breathe. I trust. He WILL breathe.

'C'mon baby, c'mon!' Tamara calls him in, rubbing and flipping him like a rag doll. Paul and I watch, frozen. Gemma-Rose's camera goes clickety-click, capturing every moment, but she respects my boundary and I still can't see her. I observe, in slow motion, the calm yet urgent activity of the midwives. Tamara and her colleague negotiate next steps in synergy, using single words, no doubt wondering if it's time to hit the big red button on the wall. I imagine the emergency paediatric team flying in with their infant resus cart.

One gasp. Baby startles and throws his arms out. It disperses the tension in the room. He cries loudly and pinks up immediately.

Paul helps me out of the tub. I sit on a stool and release the placenta. I feel sore but euphoric. Adrenalized. Tamara hands the baby back to me and our hands touch in sisterly familiarity. Gemma-Rose packs her equipment, and we thank her as she says goodbye. Weeks from now she'll present me with a selection of classy black and white birth photos.

His name is Kyle. He weighs almost a kilogram more than his sister. We were expecting a bigger baby, but not a whole kilogram.

I check the clock and remind Paul that the New Mothers' Morning Tea will be wrapping up one floor above. The supervising midwife says we're free to attend, but maybe Paul should carry the baby.

We ride the elevator to Level 6. I guide Paul to the room, and we enter. The last few guests are leaving and today's host, Dani, is stacking chairs. She lights up with surprise when she sees us and asks me how everything went. I'm still feeling good, and stupidly chuffed, that I managed to bring our baby to morning tea.

But that changes quickly. Suddenly, I don't feel so great. I'm standing here and wondering why. The room swims and I feel faint.

I stammer, 'Dani, can I have a chair?'

She drags one over and I ease myself down. 'My God,' she says, 'I forgot you only gave birth an hour ago!'

I've showed off enough. I tell Paul I don't think I should walk back. When he wheels me back to the Birth Centre, the midwives in the tearoom giggle that they thought I might be overdoing it, but they rightly let me decide.

'No more strain for the rest of the day, okay?' says Karen.

'Does that mean we can go?' I ask.

'The paediatricians on his way.'

We wait for the well-baby check that will discharge Kyle so we can take him home.

Paul and I collect big brother and sister from the sitter and return home to our bubble. We've three weeks parental leave, and this time we have a plan.

First, Paul breaks down the base of our bed and lays the mattress on the floor. We take the mattress from the cot in the next room and wedge it next to our mattress. Fortunately, they're the same height with no significant crevice between. Paul brings in a spare single mattress as a temporary bed for himself, or the children, if we should spill over and need more sleeping space. This is about getting through the sleepless early weeks, as Elijah and Ruby are still waking at night and will need us as much as they always have. I berate myself for not being open to co-sleeping when they were tiny babies. So many hours spent alone on a chair in the dark, breastfeeding with morbid thoughts, when really, I just wanted to cuddle and sleep.

Kyle's birth brings a slower, juicier, rhythm to our family. I like it a lot. It's a blessing that Elijah and Ruby have accepted him, and now that Ruby's a walking, talking toddler, the two play together with more imagination and less facilitation, leaving me free to lavish my mother-muse. Kyle possesses an easy-going temperament, with regular appetites and sleep cycles. We quickly find our rhythm. Paul and I spend hours marvelling at how his little arms float upward while he sleeps, as though he dreams he's weightless inside the womb.

Paul is also using his family leave to help his sister, Kay. Andrew is slowly slipping away. No one can say exactly when it might happen. He's sedated and calm. We're holding our collective breath. I think of Maddie and Felix, losing their dad so young. And of Milton, Kay's son from her first marriage, stepping into adulthood, who loves Andrew like his own father. I've a newborn and two hectic children. I'm incapable of leaning in to support Kay in her hardship and she doesn't ask me to.

14 A GOOD DEATH

July 2003

Mum requested that we not go looking for her. I can't call to tell her that Kyle has arrived. So, I call her friend Bethany, who I suspect knows Mum's whereabouts, and ask her to relay the news. I have to admit, I'm not ready to see Mum either. I can forgive her for what she did. But not for how she did it.

Driving back from our one-week postnatal visit at the Birth Centre, Paul's phone rings. He pulls over to answer. I can tell by his face it's Kay.

I lean in and he nods. I know what this means. We talked this morning about how it could be soon.

The only thing he says is, 'When?'

I can hear Kay's voice on Paul's phone, but I can't make out words. He hangs up.

'We need to detour to Kay's house.' Paul knows I won't object. 'The undertaker is coming to take Andrew. The kids are with the counsellors at St Vincent's and on their way to say last goodbyes.'

I imagine being Kay, at home alone with my recently deceased husband.

I stammer, 'I don't think I'll be much help.'

'It's all right,' he puts his hand on my arm. 'There's nothing you can do. Wait in the car with Kyle. We're just not sure how long they'll be, is all.'

I watch from the street as Maddie and Felix arrive with a minder from the palliative care team. She takes them inside the house. Then an ambulance arrives, no lights or sirens required, and a stretcher is taken upstairs. The children come out to the garden again, still young enough to play on the swing while they wait. Then, a few minutes later, the stretcher returns. A vinyl bag covers Andrew, so small it's hard to believe he was once such a tall and handsome man. There are tight straps holding everything in place as they navigate the stairs and the garden gate back to the ambulance. I look back at our one-week old baby strapped in the capsule in our back seat, sleeping peacefully. But I don't cry. There are no tears for this.

The ancients were buried with their possessions or burned on a pyre or covered by a cairn of stones. Our ancestors' funerals were informal affairs, conducted at home without wreaths or flowers, maybe even without a priest or a coffin. The community would have catered a wake, and delivered meals beyond that, leaving the family free to grieve without the burden of feeding their guests. Today we wouldn't dream of having a funeral in our home. We outsource all that and the catering too, and even the final ritual of saying goodbye – the washing and dressing and touching that gives catharsis to loved ones left behind.

Whatever happens in the space between, every sentient being learns there's a beginning and there'll be an end. Birth and death are the inescapable rites of passage that rub our humanity raw. Yet we've abandoned both – relegating them to hospitals, hospices, palliative services, funeral homes, and churches.

Our cultural ideal of what constitutes a 'good death' is defined by place. Home is where we can most be ourselves, feel safe and unobserved, with all our familiar comforts, and where our family and friends are most likely to feel at peace with our departure. Where they can hold the space.

Throughout history and across cultures, working with the dying has traditionally fallen to midwives. For millennia, they escorted life in and out of this world with the same sensitive energy, not just for the birthing or the dying, but also for their family and community. Souls enter this world and then they let go. The quiet presence of a compassionate midwife has the potential to facilitate magic. No wonder people once called them witches. Sometimes they still do.

Paul's parental leave is over too soon. He returns to work and I return to checking my email and reading the forums. Without Paul around, the house quickly returns to its sticky, smeary, toddler disorder. I contemplate getting back to play group and other activities we used to do, but now I'm mindful of not over-committing my time. Emotionally, I'm spread about as thin as I've ever been. Elijah no longer naps unless we take a long drive, and the routines of three tiny people are just easier to manage at home. So, at home we stay.

I still have our reliable sitter to lean on when I have complex errands. I've forgone our cleaner to afford the luxury of childcare more often. And I've returned to Maternity Coalition meetings to learn from the other advocates, which ultimately helps FBC be a more effective group. Having a reliable day-care situation means I'm less concerned about overloading the children. At least the cost of childcare is not something Paul and I argue about. He never expected that volunteering would be free. Parking costs money. Petrol costs money. Childcare costs money. I can pursue my passion and he willingly absorbs the expense. He calls it his social contribution.

15 GENIUS

September 2003

I drive up the winding mountain road to Bruce Teakle's house for the inaugural pizza party of the new Maternity Coalition. All the birth reform alliances in our state: Friends of the Birth Centre, Home Midwifery Association, The Australian College of Midwives, The Childbirth Education Association, and others, can now collectively liaise under one umbrella.

BAD ROAD, LAST CHANCE, TURN BACK, says the sign in capital letters. It sounds like a threat. Or a challenge. I'm audacious enough to arrive early and drive myself, and two-month-old Kyle, several hundred metres through the rainforest to the yard below.

To the untrained eye, Bruce Teakle and his wife, Erika Hobba, could be mistaken for hillbillies. But to those who know them, they're one of the many guises of genius.

Their house is unconventional, made from timber, corrugated iron, and traditional whitewashed wattle and daub that are every bit in harmony with the productive food garden and the forest in the gully below. I extract Kyle from his car seat, and we head inside where Erika is chopping onions.

A huge tub of dough proves by the woodstove and a tub of passata on the bench fills the room with an aroma of garlic and herbs. Bruce retreats to the garden to check the fire in the pizza dome. I lay out my cheese and salami. Every guest is to bring a topping.

Inside, the house is compact but open plan with handmade timber furniture and reclaimed wooden casement windows. There's an austere beauty here that makes the materials irrelevant. It's well-maintained with plenty of light. Charming, uncluttered, solid and warm. I've never seen a lovelier family home.

I notice there's no TV.

My children, still so young, have favourite programs and movies already. But Bruce and Erika's two, Harry and Matilda, have no concept of syndicated entertainment. They play. They walk around with sticks and explore the woods and creeks. They sometimes come home with leeches or bush mites called 'scrub itch' after sitting on the ground or brushing against some vegetation.

'What led you and Bruce to homebirth, Erika, for your first baby and all?' I can't contain my curiosity. 'I would never have been so brave.'

Bruce pokes his head through the window. 'It was purely Erika's decision and I supported her,' which makes us laugh.

'It wasn't brave,' she says, 'and I don't recall a *decision*.'

She emphasises the word like it's a foreign language.

'Connecting with a midwife was easy. My sister had her baby the year before. For me, living this way,' she gestures toward the airy room and out the window to the land, 'it was a normal and natural thing to do.'

'You wouldn't have a baby in a hospital?' I'm fishing for the boundary.

'If necessary. But I was a healthy woman with a healthy pregnancy. Why would I need a hospital?'

'No ultrasound?'

'There's no evidence they improve outcomes for mothers and babies, overall. My midwife detected a healthy heartbeat and a high placenta. If there was a problem, she'd have conferred with me and her colleagues on a course of action. That might have meant transfer to hospital for tests or interventions. As it was, I didn't need to. Harry was born right there,' she points, 'in a tub we set up in our living room.'

She chops another onion. 'Matilda's birth was almost exactly the same. If I have another baby though, I'll have to find a new midwife.'

'Oh?' I know so little about homebirth. I'm mindful of not asking a question that might offend my host. 'How do you know they're competent if they work outside a hospital?'

'If they're self-employed?' Erika gives me a quizzical look. Clearly, I don't understand how this works.

Bruce returns to the table and pours a glass of home-made lemonade. He offers me one as he sits. 'Have you heard of a midwife called Claire Brassard?'

I shake my head. I can tell he has told this story before.

'This all started for us when a couple, clients of Claire's, called us wanting to support her because she was being investigated by the Queensland Nursing Council. They oversee the conduct of the nursing and midwifery profession in Queensland. Claire was our midwife too, so they got our attention. She was a certified and practising midwife in Montreal, before she came to Australia. She became one of Brisbane's best-known independent midwives.'

Bruce continues. 'It went awry for her around 2000 when a client had an undetected twin. It's rare, but it happens, especially since some women decline an ultrasound scan – which is their right, I might add.'

I sip my lemonade, listening.

'The first baby was born, no problems at all. The mother experienced some complications, so they transferred her to hospital. There, they realised there was a second baby that wasn't doing well. Someone in Queensland Health lodged a complaint with the Nursing Council, questioning Claire's right to practice.'

'But, you see,' adds Bruce, pointing a finger, 'the word *midwife* is a protected title, and you must meet your state's criteria to practise. Queensland law can't recognise Claire's qualifications as a midwife because no bridging course exists to prove her credentials. To meet the criteria, she would first have to become a nurse, and then specialise in midwifery. She didn't need to be a nurse, and she couldn't easily leave her home to study interstate.'

Bruce shakes his head, 'So we formed Brisbane Birth Action Group to lobby for a process to recognise the skills of midwives separate to nursing, and guarantee women's access to midwifery care. Kerry, Cesca and Sarah are coming today, and others who worked with us then. They knew the court case would crush Claire's career and if anything was ever going to change for midwives, we should put on a grand show of support.'

Erika says, 'We expected the press to present it like a witch hunt. Instead, we treated her like The Queen.'

'Did she win?' I ask.

Bruce gives me a patient sideways glance. 'There was no way she could win, or even challenge the Nursing Council,' he says. 'Regardless of her experience or skill, Claire was not, and had never been, a registered midwife in Australia. There's no mechanism in Queensland by which she can demonstrate her competency. So now she studies midwifery in New Zealand. Three year's study. This is a mature woman, almost sixty years of age, a midwife from Quebec.'

Erika becomes animated. 'We presented her with a huge bunch of roses as she left the courthouse and got a beautiful picture in the paper. It took weeks of work to get that picture, making phone calls, writing press releases, ensuring people would come and support her on the day.'

A chatter of people approaches from the driveway. Bruce leans in for the punchline.

'Afterwards, we gathered at Kerry McGovern's house to celebrate. We thought it was over. Then she said, "Next, we call the health writer at *The Courier-Mail* to suggest an article. Then we get all the mothers from HMA to visit their local members.

You've got to keep the conversation going, Bruce. Give it at least two years." It's been two years and now I can see it'll take five.' Bruce throws his head back with a laugh. 'Maybe ten.' He plonks his empty lemonade glass down on the table and walks up the yard to greet his guests.

The pizzas come with a range of exotic toppings. Everything is delicious. I meet a whirl of names and faces and it'll take time for my placenta brain to integrate them all. Dr Sarah Buckley kisses my cheek and congratulates me on baby Kyle, who was still in my belly when we last met.

Bruce introduces me to Kerry McGovern. She's fair and youthful, with sparkling eyes; a fast talker with a head for numbers.

She leans in and shakes my hand. 'I saw your segment on Channel Seven.'

'I was awkward,' I reply, embarrassed.

Kerry tells me she's one of the founders of the Home Midwifery Association in Brisbane, who'd encouraged Claire Brassard to come to Australia and practice as their sage-femme. She'd collaborated with other mothers and midwives to write the HOME program, a policy document for independent midwives. It encouraged midwives to collaborate, debrief and share skills, and keep impeccable records. Kerry once worked for the Treasury with insight into the health budget under Joh Bjelke-Petersen.

'Bruce and I met with the Health Minister, several times. She came from a medical family and was never in favour of homebirth. Hopefully, she'll retire soon.'

'That would be bloody brilliant!' says irreverent midwife, Jenny Gamble. 'When are we going to stop telling women how to birth? We've got all the evidence that home is safe, and midwives do it better. Fucking compelling evidence. But with hospitals, there's so much complexity, and of course, the budget. They aren't improving how they work with women beyond offering friendlier C-sections.'

'You had visiting rights at the Mater,' I say. 'Obstetricians supported you?'

'Yes, three of them, for a while, with my work partner, Jenny Fenwick. They called us *The Two Jennies*. But then they dropped us like a hot potato. Obstetricians can't generate an income working with midwives. We're an inconvenience to them.'

It's interesting, the power struggles surrounding birth. The developed world looks to technology to rescue women from their pain and keep babies safe, when statistically, technology harms as many as it rescues. What messages are we telling girls about their bodies? What messages are we failing to tell them? How can hospitals do birth better and kinder? I can't sit back feeling grateful for my lovely births without trying to improve it for others.

16 PUTTING DOWN ROOTS

October 2003

I glance in the rear-view mirror. The kids look happily occupied. We're off to the hospital for this month's Mothers' Morning Tea, which for them is like going to play group because there'll be lots of other children to play with.

Stopped at the traffic lights, I interject, 'Hey kids, look!' and point to a mother and baby on the crossing. The baby has our t-shirt, the one that says A Midwife Helped Me Out. My kids are wearing them too. It's our uniform for all Birth Centre activities. I've never seen this woman before. It's satisfying to know there are other mothers proudly dressing their babies in our shirts. Happy customers.

I use the parking station because the free parking is several blocks away, and that's too far to hike with two toddlers and a baby. I waddle like a duck through the hospital corridors leading the children by hand and wearing a baby sling. We ride the elevator, the children giggle as it drops and rises, to the meeting room on the sixth floor. Hannah is hosting this month. She has set up a circle of chairs around the room, and a corner with toys. Prams are parked in the centre of the room. A trestle at the far end will hold whatever food today's group can bring. An electric urn, bought with a small community grant, is bubbling in the corner. Today, we expect about forty women to attend.

Hannah welcomes the group and tells the story of how she found the Birth Centre and subsequently joined FBC. She hands over to me to explain how our core goal is to support and promote the Birth Centre. Usually, a few midwives pop in to say hello, share a cup of tea and cuddle some babies.

Women tell us their stories, how they heard about the Birth Centre, how they felt during their prenatal visits, who their midwives were, and whatever birth details they want to share or debrief about.

One woman is not yet pregnant. She introduces herself as Melissa Fox. She works in documentary film making and she's here to research her options. I'm impressed that this young woman will not be tripping over her birth choices like so many of us. I'm happy to answer her questions. Melissa takes a membership form, but I don't expect to see her again.

The Home Midwifery Association meets at a cottage in Windsor owned by the Sisters of Mercy. It's close to the hospital and I check out their home base with envy. There's a kitchen, a bathroom, and a playground in the backyard. I settle the children in to play where there are minders watching the yard. Baby Kyle comes inside with me.

The convenor, Angie, greets me with a hug. We've only exchanged emails before today. The format is not like a committee meeting. This is a support circle. The women sit on the floor or on the furniture that circles the walls, with an open space in the centre where babies can crawl.

Angie calls everyone to start and welcomes new members, including me. Everyone takes turns around the room, updating the circle on their lives since they last met. Even with regular reminders to 'keep it short' this process takes an hour or more. Someone asks a question, or the speaker takes a tangent.

Often, discussion escalates to everyone talking at once, until Angie brings them back to order.

After everyone has spoken, I feel bonded to these women, even if I can't remember their names. There's usually a guest presenter, or a discussion topic or activity for the second half of the gathering, then everyone lays out assorted goodies for lunch, all home-made. Many women are braless, with natural hair, and I recognise a depth in them that goes beyond appearance. I continue to attend their monthly circles and become expert at baking banana bread.

17 THE MOST IMPORTANT MEAL OF THE DAY

November 2003

Paul waves at me from the kitchen with a slotted spoon.

'One egg or two?'

He's working from home today and looking relaxed in blue jeans and a polo shirt. Today, for once, I'm setting the pace.

'Sorry, no time.' I bustle down the hallway, my hair wrapped in a towel. Kyle is on a blanket on the living room floor, entertained by his brother and sister. 'I dallied in the shower.'

'C'mon, it was worth it, right?'

I kiss him on the cheek and glance at the clock on the wall, 'Yes, but Bruce will be here any minute.' We have a meeting in the city with Queensland Health. I unwrap my hair and give my new short cut a flick. I won't get to dry it before we go.

'It's the most important meal of the day.' He points at a glass of water on the bench, 'That's for you, and it's not like Bruce has never seen you eat.'

I gulp down the whole glass with impatience and square it on the bench with a thud. At the same time a rap at the door declares that Bruce is here. Punctual, as always.

'Come in!' Paul and I call in unison.

Bruce takes off his Akubra hat and steps inside. I introduce the two most influential men in my life.

'Nice to meet you,' Bruce offers his hand.

Paul shakes it. 'You too. Jodie has told me all about you.'

Truth be told, Paul is rather tired of hearing me talk about Bruce and Erika and their low technology lifestyle. I recall the disbelief my energy-junkie husband expressed when I described their single photo-voltaic cell trickling to a battery that runs a fridge, a freezer, some lights and a single laptop computer.

'Thanks to Jodie for driving us today. Saves riding the buses.'

Paul cocks his head, 'You don't drive?'

'I have a ute, but I try to take the bus as much as possible. Public transport, use it or lose it!' A gentle lisp is audible as he pronounces the sibilants.

I was going to leave Kyle with Paul, but Bruce insisted I bring him along.

Paul scoops an egg from the saucepan, 'Would you like some, Bruce?'

'I'm all good, thanks. I try not to leave the house without breakfast. It's the most important meal of the day!'

Paul shoots me a look and places a plate with two poached eggs on toast before me. 'How does it work,' Paul asks, 'a man selling homebirth?' I cringe that he would ask such a blokey question. Bruce doesn't skip a beat.

He says, 'People generally don't know what to make of me. Some people still defer matters of policy to men.'

I chime in, 'Women at this stage of life can't sacrifice their family time.'

'Exactly,' says Bruce, 'But I bring women along to every meeting. It's best if they have a baby or a belly. I can't be effective without them.'

'How does your family afford you to do this, Bruce?'

'Paul!' How could he even ask?

Bruce shrugs, 'We get the family allowance like everyone else, and have learnt how to be frugal so we can do what's important to us.'

Paul is scandalised by the idea. And yet, I see nothing wrong with Bruce living on public money while he advocates for women and midwives. How is it different to bureaucrats in their government jobs? It would appear Bruce is much more efficient at getting things done.

We park on Charlotte Street, close to the offices of Queensland Health. We'll meet Cesca and Debby outside. Cesca will represent the homebirth community and Debby, the support group, Birthtalk, giving women who've had a traumatic birth a safe space to unpack their stories.

Bruce gave me a summary of the process during our drive but, as a first timer, I still don't really know what to expect.

As convenor for Friends of the Birth Centre, I represent some 200 families who've used the Birth Centre and subsequently joined our consumer group. I also represent countless women in Queensland who would choose care with a known midwife, if such a thing existed in their health district.

Currently, around one percent of pregnant women in Australia can access a Birth Centre, and birthing services in regional hospitals are closing at an alarming rate. The ballooning ballot at the Royal demonstrates an unmet need. When I tell people about the Birth Centre, they love the idea. Who doesn't want the comfort of a family-centred birth space – a double bed, sofa, and a home-like decor, with medical equipment out of sight? Don't we all want to see the same friendly person who provided our prenatal care, once labour has begun?

Cesca and Debby are waiting for us. Our greetings are brief – we're all keen to head inside. Bruce has done some homework on the woman we're to meet. She's a middle manager at Queensland Health and a grandmother who was once a nurse. He says she's not a decision-maker but may have influence up the chain. She may also be willing to share her expertise with us as we plan a campaign for next year's State election.

We sign in and receive our visitor badges. In the waiting area, Kyle, now four months old, entertains us by blowing bubbles.

Change in maternity services won't happen without good advocacy, but parents of babies and small children are at a disadvantage; too busy to help themselves. Bruce says the baby has a job today. He's to breastfeed and require nappy changes and remind everyone about the realities of parenting. Politicians and health executives are usually mothers and fathers, too. If they aren't, the baby is to be their education.

We meet our public servant and shake hands. Bruce begins with polite questions about her role in the health sector. Somehow, through a process of friendly banter, he asks who reports to her, who does she report to, and how far does her influence reach?

I introduce myself as the president of Friends of the Birth Centre Association and Kyle as my third water-born baby with the same midwife. I tell her how overwhelmingly satisfied I was with this arrangement, about the growing FBC membership and the ballooning waiting list for the service that resulted in our very polite demonstration in King George Square.

'Ah yes, I remember it,' she confirms. 'Well done.'

A tiny shiver of satisfaction interrupts my train of thought. If she remembers, then hopefully her superiors are aware of it too?

'We in FBC don't understand why services like Birth Centres, with such excellent outcomes, low caesarean rates and high breastfeeding rates, aren't in every hospital.'

Cesca speaks next, telling the story of her homebirth in Melbourne, and how hard it was to find an independent midwife in Brisbane – and that was years ago, before the insurance crisis. 'There will always be women who choose homebirth. Hospitals don't support the hormonal physiology of birth. We need to protect independent midwives who serve these women and keep them and their babies safe.'

The woman lifts an eyebrow but keeps her mouth tightly closed. Does she support the ideas we present? I can't tell.

Debby follows, explaining why she and her sister-in-law started Birthtalk. The women in Birthtalk always go on to have empowered births, often with the added expense of a doula or a private midwife which they can't access through their hospital. Many stay home to give birth where they feel more comfortable and in control.

Our host asks Debby, 'And what's your stance on these women who won't go to hospital?'

'In my experience, they avoid the hospital for valid reasons. They need a completely different experience to what they had the first time. If midwives can work in the home and serve the needs of these mothers and babies, there's a safety net.'

The woman listens respectfully and asks pertinent questions while being blunt with us about the obstacles. She knows the system is not meeting these needs but doesn't know what she can do to help.

She asks, 'Have you spoken with Wendy Edmonds about this?'

Bruce lights up. 'We've met with the Health Minister, yes, several times. She has been, how shall I put it...'

'Hostile?'

Bruce's cheek twitches but he remains diplomatic, 'We had a deputation to meet with her and the Parliamentary Secretary, as well as the Director General. They were dismissive.

'Wendy's preparing to retire at the next election. There's a chance her replacement will be...' she trails off.

'...more receptive?' Bruce finishes for her. We receive this nugget with gratitude. Kerry's prediction was right.

'What about the Chief Health Officer?' The woman is testing Bruce.

'Bryan Campbell? He listened patiently and told us we were asking for Rolls Royce care on a Toyota budget.'

'Is it true?'

'That it costs more to start care with midwives?' She looks like she might already know the health economics of primary midwifery care.

'The opposite,' says Bruce. 'The Royal drilled down and maternity care in the Birth Centre costs half that of active management on the ward.'

She shakes our hands and promises to look into it. I leave with the sense that she's a powerless pen pusher, but Bruce is less dismissive.

'You never know who will see an opportunity and step up and advocate. One evening I received an anonymous phone call from someone who said they worked at Queensland Health. She encouraged me to keep harassing them. She said it won't look like you're making a difference, but trust that you are. I took that as permission to bother the heck out of everyone.'

Bruce probably baffles the public servants. Here is a farmer-type in his beat-up Akubra with dirt under his fingernails, talking about having babies with midwives and the inequity of the laws and policies that surround it. I think they under-estimate Bruce, and he happily exploits that. The health executives and office bearers and members of parliament who meet their 'serial letter writer' and shake his hand, are then caught by surprise having a real conversation about what's going on within public and private hospitals. He asks for their professional advice and listens to what they have to say before posing an even more pertinent question. Like it or not, they form a respectful relationship. He follows up with a letter, always asking for a reply. He answers their reply with another letter, another phone call, and sometimes another meeting, asking for representation on this matter, and the cycle continues. Some of his targets now know him so well, their acquaintance borders on friendship.

18 BIRTH MAGIC

Late November 2003

I cross the threshold of Windsor House for Home Midwifery Association's monthly support circle. The room feels overly warm, so louvres are opened, and furniture is shifted. When the chairs and couches are full, women gravitate to the floor to breastfeed as the 'What's on Top?' question is sent around the room. It feels like an unusually large group today.

Jessica introduces herself. She's a young single mother seeking a midwife. Her tummy looks like she's maybe six months along and although she's healthy, she's deemed to be a risk because of her youth, single status, and perhaps her strong will rubs hospital staff the wrong way. I admire the confidence of these young women who know how they want to give birth. I was never like them.

I go next, introducing myself as I always do.

'My name is Jodie, married, with three babies all born in water at the Royal's Birth Centre. I also convene Friends of the Birth Centre and I advocate with Maternity Coalition. I'm here to learn more about homebirth.'

On the couch, a woman named Anouk introduces herself but doesn't say much more. She's in her late forties and wears her hair long and naturally grey. Lined eyes and weathered skin reveal a life spent under the Australian sun. Beside her is a very pregnant dark-haired woman. She calls herself Venus and explains that birth is imminent for her sixth baby. She can't afford a midwife and can't secure one anyway due to her age and multi-gravida status.

'What's on top?' she says. 'It's all on top. I don't have a partner to help with my kids. This is the father's first baby. He's barely older than my oldest child, so not much use with the kids. I know what this looks like. Believe me, I feel ashamed.' She stops and gulps air to stop herself crying. Anouk, despite her tough appearance, reaches out her hand and places it supportively on the woman's knee. Someone nearby passes a tissue.

Venus breathes deep and continues. She has not seen a GP, or a midwife. Her prenatal care has been the occasional vitamin pill when she remembers to take it. She has avoided setting foot in a hospital as she has a mental health record that she worries might bias her care provider.

She confesses her house is a mess and worries that Child Services might come knocking on her door. Because she can't hire a midwife, she's choosing to give birth at home without one. Despite the hormonal tears, in a room full of women who've opted out of the system, she seems perfectly rational to me. I say, 'Could you turn up at Emergency, ready to push?'

Anouk shoots me a look. I've crossed a line.

'Are you telling her what to do? You aren't her. Your middle-class babies were born at the middle-class Birth Centre. It's potluck for everyone else.' A murmur becomes audible in the room, like the hum of a swarm of bees.

'Women are sick of handing over their power. Have we forgotten what we're capable of? Soon as there's a professional in the room, women disconnect from themselves and their bodies and submit to the doctor or midwife. When will the establishment start asking women what they want instead of telling them to 'get up on the bed, put your feet in these stirrups, and be quiet. Everyone can hear you, silly girl?''

A braver woman than me speaks up, 'And what will you do if something goes wrong?'

Venus speaks for herself. 'Right now, I can't afford to put my head there. I can't access anything like the Birth Centre. They call me high-risk. I'm not.' She beats her chest with the flat of her palm. 'I'm a woman having a normal pregnancy. It just so happens that I'm forty-five and have been pregnant a few times before. Some of those births were in hospitals and wholly unpleasant affairs.'

Anouk beside her nods her head.

'Doctors don't listen to people like me,' Venus continues. 'They see my psych file and I lose my voice.' She chokes and a tear trickles down her cheek.

Another woman in the group tries to soothe Venus, but she isn't finished. 'When I cry people ask if I'm seeing someone. A psychologist or a social worker. I'm allowed to cry. I'm sorry my tears make you uncomfortable, but that's not my problem.'

All the compassionate women sitting by Venus reach out and touch her arm, her shoulder, her knee. They silently give her permission to weep until the emotion has passed. This is not something I've witnessed at FBC. We have such different cultures. Anouk takes her turn to soapbox.

'It's not illegal to give birth. It's her body and her baby.' I gather that Anouk supported other women in this room to freebirth. She clearly has status here.

'If women can't terminate an unwanted pregnancy, what rights do we have at the other end of the spectrum when the baby is to be born? It's not a legal person until the moment of birth. Taking all emotion away, it's an organ in my body.'

The room is silent. My heart is beating so hard I can hear it.

Venus finishes for herself, 'I trust my body to do its job when the time comes. And I *will* love this baby.'

In her shoes, I might have made the same decision. I can feel the weight of where she is. After the circle I ask if I can help. Maybe cook some meals for her large family. She receives my offer gratefully and gives me her address.

I cook a huge shepherd's pie and a pasta bake and freeze them, wondering when to deliver. I forgot to ask Venus when her baby is due.

Weeks later, I'm trying to make space in the freezer. The kids are cranky with the heat and need to sleep. I take the slip of paper off the fridge with Venus's address and decide to drive those huge trays of food all the way to where she lives on the south-west outskirts of Brisbane. As I rattle down the long driveway of her rural property in the crook of the Brisbane River, there's Anouk walking across the lawn, holding a coffee mug. She looks at me with suspicion and strides in my direction, then recognition flashes in her eyes. I park and step out of the car, leaving it to idle since the children are still asleep in the air conditioning. I brandish the two frozen dinners in their chiller bag.

'I figure Venus is due about now. Here are some dinners ready to go. Two meals for ten people.'

Anouk accepts the bag with her free hand. 'Venus gave birth five minutes ago. This sweet tea is for her.'

She gestures with the mug towards what looks like a greenhouse. All the windows have blankets hanging like curtains, presumably to block out the light.

'Everything went well?' It feels like none of my business.

'She took her time,' Anouk says, 'and did it hard towards the end, but she's good now. Bub's feeding.'

I don't ask for more information: boy or girl, placenta passed? No haemorrhaging, I hope – a genuine risk for a grand multi, the risk of bleeding to death if the uterus won't contract after the placenta comes away. Or a prolapse where the uterus slumps to the bottom of the abdominal cavity, or worse, is expelled with the baby.

'She won't remember me but tell her congratulations.'

I turn to leave. Anouk resumes her walk with my insulated freezer bag. I close the car door as quietly as I can and drive away.

19 SQUEEZED OUT LIKE TOOTHPASTE

December 2003

It has been five months and finally, here is Mum, sitting at my kitchen bench, sharing a pot of tea. Her friend, whom I've been calling now and then, did all the organising and driving and speaking for her today. Mum has barely said a word except, 'I'm not talking about it, so don't ask.'

So, I don't.

Instead, I introduce her to Kyle, and bring Elijah and Ruby for cuddles while I talk to fill the awkward silence. I tell her how the reunion went without a hitch, how Andrew died soon after Kyle was born, how I've been sitting on a committee to review waterbirth policy at the Royal. And our big news – we've bought a block of land a half hour out of town.

'That's nice, dear,' she says.

I want to talk to Mum alone. By the end, we still haven't had a meaningful exchange about what's going on for her. She looks thin. I hope she's all right.

Today, Cesca is hosting the Maternity Coalition meeting at her house in West End. Her street is narrow with parking permitted on one side only. But the parking gods are smiling and I luck a spot close enough that the walk in the heat, with a baby and all his accessories, won't raise a sweat. I enter her gate where the Geraldton Wax is blooming, climb the steps to her open front door and call, 'Hello?' because my hands are too full to knock.

I hear her walk barefoot across the timber floor of the pre-war cottage. She pokes her head around the corner and beckons me in. She's a classic beauty; tall and slim, with olive skin, auburn hair and dark brown eyes.

'I'm sorry, Jodie, isn't it? I'm not quite ready,' she's rifling through a laundry hamper, looking harried. 'Forgive the kitchen. My daughter called to remind me to wash her netball uniform for tonight. People think we volunteer because we've so much time on our hands.'

Cesca's girls are 8 and 14 years old. She works in the city as a program coordinator for Kids Helpline. She's had to rearrange her day for this, so I let her get on with her laundry mission. I put Kyle on the floor so my hands can be free.

The dishes in the sink don't matter. My kitchen looks the same. We just need paper towels, coffee cups, and some glasses for water. I fill the kettle and push the button so hot water will be ready when everyone comes. This ritual of meeting in each other's homes fosters a familiarity that's slowly building a solid community.

Soon all the regulars enter Cesca's front door, helping themselves to tea and coffee. Jocelyn Toohill, a midwife from the Mater Mothers, Dr Sarah Buckley and Jenny Gamble, and many others, midwives and social workers and mothers I met at the pizza party. Bruce and Erika have brought four-year-old Matilda. We take our seats around Cesca's enormous vintage table, her family photos laid out on the surface under a pane of glass. Attending: sixteen adults, plus their little people, and more to come. But it's time to start.

Bruce opens the meeting. 'Now that we're working with the national committee, there's a lot to talk about.'

It's inspiring that so many across the country are coordinating on what ought to be a mainstream issue. Half the

Australian population are women, with a median age of thirty-eight. A majority of those are women with children.

Bruce summarises his recent meetings with Members of Parliament, government officials or health executives and where they fit into the chain of influence. His observations are needle sharp and respectful, belying an irreverent sense of humour.

Kerry adds, 'I heard there might be an early election.'

The Queensland Premier, Peter Beattie, is in the public good books for his Smart State initiative, which has attracted and retained tech talent in Queensland – including the software company my husband works for, and his international team.

'Peter's wife, Heather, is a nurse educator and academic,' Kerry continues, 'and they have three children.' Bruce's face lights up, 'They might discuss maternity matters over the breakfast table.'

Kerry nods. 'I know them well enough to bend Peter's ear. So, I invited Heather to meet with Maternity Coalition.' Someone volunteers her home for a venue, and we all promise to turn up and tell our stories.

Cesca also has a gem of information. 'A friend at Channel Nine says that, tomorrow, a Sydney doctor will perform caesarean surgery on the Today show. Delivering Australia's 20 millionth citizen.'

Dissent and disapproval ripple through the group.

'So,' Cesca continues, 'spread the word through your networks to tune in and bombard them with feedback.'

After the meeting, we wash Cesca's dishes and vent our outrage about what passes for entertainment these days. Channel Nine better get ready for an ambush.

I start as soon as I get home.

I post to my community on *Natural Parenting*, pitching for members to watch the segment and call the switchboard at the number below. Such requests, to support a cause, sign a petition, write an email, or make a phone call, are well-received on the forum. It won't take an army to jam the phone lines, and all the birth advocates around Australia will follow suit.

The next day I press RECORD on my video player. If I'm to write something, I may need to view the segment again. The word 'hysterical' simmers under every issue woman raise about reproductive matters, so I'm mindful to remain calm, orderly and logical, even when parenting duties feel like none of those things.

The segment begins. Tracy Grimshaw waits excitedly at North Shore Private Hospital in Sydney. She explains what makes this, the birth of today's one in 1,400 babies, significant to the arrival of Australia's 20 millionth citizen. She reassures the audience that 'they're going to see a miracle, not gore.' 'Magic,' she adds. 'We're going to see a marvellous moment in life!'

Dr Ric Gordon, who'll perform the surgery, explains the difference between the various anaesthesia. Tracy asks awkward questions, revealing she's unfamiliar with the procedures. Dr Gordon says, 'We'll get the mother positioned, put a whole lot of drapes over her, prepare the area with some antiseptic solution, and it's on for young and old.'

The doctor appears well-spoken and good looking enough for television. His surgical mask hangs casually around his neck so we can see his face. It's easy to miss that there's a woman in the room around whom this spectacle revolves. Mum, Leanne, consenting to this procedure, sits upright and hugging a pillow, awaiting her spinal block. No doubt she can hear the discussion being conducted about her, for the info-tainment of the Australian viewing masses. A man standing before her in scrubs, presumably her husband, looks every bit the nervous father-to-be on national breakfast television.

Dr Gordon explains that once the spinal block takes effect they'll remove the scar tissue from her previous caesarean, and then go down through the multiple layers until they get to the uterus itself, where they'll make a small-little incision [sic] and presumably be able to see the baby's head. The word 'cut' is conspicuous by its absence.

After that, Dr Gordon tells us he'll reach in and bring the baby's head up into the wound where his doctor-colleague, 'will apply a little bit of pressure from above and out will come baby, squeezed out like toothpaste'. Nervous laughter pervades the room. Grimshaw interjects, 'Sound good, Leanne?' to which the mother nervously replies, 'Sounds great!' Tracy and Dr Ric continue to minimise her experience with Leanne awkwardly out of shot.

Compere Steve Liebmann segues to a studio interview with midwife, Andrea Robertson – founder of Birth International and my beloved *Ozmidwifery* – to present the other side of the debate. Caesarean is major abdominal surgery with risks for mothers and babies. They discuss the modern reliance on surgical birth for legal reasons, even though major surgery is not without risk. Obstetricians are losing clinical skills as a result. Time runs out, but I'm satisfied that Channel Nine have attempted to balance their presentation of a beautiful birth with some ugly facts.

When we return to the operating room, Dr Gordon has almost completed the lower half incision, through layers of skin, then fat, then uterus. They check on the mother's comfort with the procedure while they complete the final incision and Dr Gordon announces, 'here come the waters, Trace,' to the sound of trickling fluid, though maybe the parents would have liked to be in on it, too? Tracy exclaims, 'Wow!' to the sound of suctioning.

Dr Gordon warns Leanne there'll be 'a little bit of pushing on your tummy, all right?' and Tracy is agog at what's occurring behind the curtain that viewers cannot see. What viewers *can* see is the enormous effort to extract the baby. Doctor Ric and his assistant hunch forward and lead with their shoulders. The camera is trained on Tracy Grimshaw, like the parents are not in the room.

The doctor declares the baby's gender to the room – not the parents. Baby releases a healthy cry, they cut the cord immediately, then Dr Gordon takes the newborn away to receive some oxygen. The doctors are occupied with the next stage of the procedure, which they don't explain to us. Compere, Steve, asks Tracy if she's okay. How did she come through all this? To which she replies, 'I'm only just okay. It's very hard to stay composed.' Everyone else in the room seems more important than the mother. Birth was done to her.

They present it as an informed choice that Leanne allowed her caesarean to be televised. A great number of young women in Australia will have watched today's program. Will they have understood the respective risks and benefits of choosing a caesarean?

Finally, they swaddle the baby and place him on his mother's chest. Grimshaw is speechless at the *miracle* she has witnessed. The beautiful birth of Australia's 20 millionth citizen. A sweet melody plays us to the break, and throughout the replays beyond. In the recovery room, Dr Gordon reminds us that caesarean section is not a choice taken lightly. He reasserts this was medically indicated. Viewers have no need to question what that actually means.

Afterwards, the women of the *Natural Parenting* forum express their outrage. The birth workers on *Ozmidwifery* are doing the same. We dial the feedback line. Keyboard warriors email Channel Nine feedback. We write letters to the editor of *The Courier-Mail* and *The Sydney Morning Herald* and copy everything to ABC's *Backchat* in the hope they'll give the broadcaster a grilling.

Even the former Lord Mayor of Brisbane, Jim Soorley, uses his weekly editorial in *The Courier-Mail* to express his contempt for the gratuitous promotion of caesarean birth.

Nice to know we aren't being hysterical.

20 SUFFRAGETTES

December 2003

December 16 is the Australian centenary of women's suffrage. Three days ago, we were meeting at Cesca's table again when Kerry reminded us about this event: a Labor women's dinner in honour of the centenary.

'Isn't it crazy,' said Cesca. 'Women have had the vote for one hundred years but we still don't own our bodies?'

'And we're still just voting for a bunch of men,' said Kerry. 'Do you think this would still happen if a woman had the big chair?'

Ever the marketeer, my friend Caroline said, 'What if they had a welcoming committee?'

'Of suffragettes?' said Cesca. 'Imagine that!'

'It's three days away,' said Bruce. 'Do we have enough time?'

Kerry coordinated some black, high-waisted skirts and ruffled white blouses. The West End Theatrical Society had just staged *Mary Poppins* and owned some suitable hats, shoes and gloves. Bruce coordinated a volunteer to design a flier. Three midwives offered to wear the costumes.

In the final hours, Erika made purple and green sashes, symbols of the suffragette movement, and two delicate bamboo picket signs declaring: *I can vote – but still no rights in childbirth*, and in graphic capitals: *CHOICE IN BIRTH*. Some midwives purchased tickets to be our snitch on the inside.

So, here we wait, on the pavement of Queen Street Mall dressed as guests attending the Labor Women's Dinner. I clutch my wad of fliers. If someone objects, they might call the police. Not that we intend to be a public nuisance.

I haven't worn these nice clothes since before having babies. It's camouflage, to mingle with professional women with cocktail dresses, red lipstick and enamelled fingernails.

The purple flier features a picture of two suffragettes at a march, one pushes a pram. The flip side declares our protest.

100 Years Of The Vote but Still No Choice in Childbirth.

Women Demand Reform That Delivers:

- *Best Quality Care*
- *Informed Choice*
- *Serving OUR Needs, not doctor convenience or private profit*
- *Freely Available Statistics*
- *Local Services for Rural and Regional*
- *Our Own Choice to Birth at Birth Centre, Hospital or Home*
- *A Health Minister and Department Who Listen to Us*

A quote from one of Bruce's numerous emails drives it home.

'Thirty minutes before the birth the doctor told me that if I continued to refuse to get onto the bed and put my legs into the stirrups, I would be put into an ambulance and sent to another hospital, or he would order all staff to leave the room and my husband and I would be on our own.'

36-year-old teacher in a Brisbane public hospital, November 2003.

Dinner guests light up when they see the suffragettes, bamboo placards and all. We hand out our fliers. No one refuses them. Some guests take photos, like we're the evening's entertainment. They tell us about their daughters, and daughters-in-law, and recount their own stories. Our stooges inside report that birth reform has been the pre-dinner discussion among women of community influence. We cut through the noise. It was worth it.

A woman I haven't met before is leafleting with me. She introduces herself as Liz Leys and calls herself a doula. I've heard her name. Some call her a lay midwife, working the fringes of the alternative birth community in Brisbane. We find something to eat. Sitting at the table with Liz feels like a reunion with an old friend. She makes a motherly enquiry, for she has daughters about my age.

'How did you feel, dressing up for a night without your family?'

'My city clothes don't fit,' I say, 'and my feet are killing me.' I poke my foot out from under the table and frown at the ridiculous heels I haven't worn in years.

We giggle about that and slurp our noodles. I relax and enjoy being with Liz. I don't want to rush home just yet. She lives on a boat on the Brisbane river, so getting home is just a walk of a few blocks for her.

She asks about my babies and where they were born. I happily recount the stories of their births with Tamara at the Birth Centre.

'What about you, Liz? How did you become a doula?'

'I have five children. The youngest was born in a furious half hour, at home alone.'

I rock back in my seat. 'You weren't scared?'

'Not at all. It was the best thing in my life. When a baby comes that quickly it's likely to go well. Anyway, what could I do? Try and stop it?'

Unimaginable.

'Does three make your family complete?' She's fishing, but I don't mind. I can see why women like her.

'It would be practical to stop now, but I don't know.'

'Aha.' Liz finishes her broth with a knowing smile.

'Being around pregnant women so much, it's hard to know if we're done. Now that I've seen the other side, if I have another baby, I think I'd like to have a homebirth.'

Another baby. The idea has caught me by surprise.

21 SOMETIMES BABIES DIE

January 2004

The Queensland election has been declared for a date just three weeks away. Labor is sitting pretty, and a third term for the Beattie administration seems highly likely. The Health Minister, Wendy Edmonds, has announced her retirement. Bruce speculates about who could be the new recipient of the health portfolio, and gets ready to start over again, lobbying with a clean slate – tabula rasa.

Three mothers at the Gold Coast decided to stand as Green Party candidates, one of them is challenging a marginal seat. All of them members of the Gold Coast Homebirth Group.
I drive Bruce to the Gold Coast to attend their pep rally, which is actually more like a play group. Most of the parents seem familiar with the *National Maternity Action Plan* and its proposed pathway to maternity reform. Together they discuss the urgency of their election plans, much of which goes over my head, and I leave with Bruce in grim hope that these women might actually wield some influence. It's all over my head, so I interrogate Bruce on the long drive home.

'What chance is there that Queensland Health will endorse the NMAP? Why not just lobby for more Birth Centres in hospitals? We might have a chance of achieving that.'

'Yes, lowering our expectations would probably yield results,' says Bruce. 'Looks like Labor's position is safe, and it would make them look good to include a nice new Birth Centre in every urban hospital.'

'Birth Centres could fill that gap, though?'

'It's a pipe dream Jodie. They've tightened the definition of low risk at the Birth Centre and added conditions like compulsory ultrasound and glucose testing, and weight restrictions to use the tubs. Absolutely, putting a Birth Centre into every hospital is what we want. But midwives'll never achieve autonomy of practice that way. And women'll still want to give birth at home. Woman-centred care is incompatible with hospital-centric policy. If an elective caesarean is one end of the spectrum of choice, then access to safe birth at home has to be the other.'

I keep my eyes on the road while I drive, 'Okay, I get it.'

'When we formed Brisbane Birth Action Group,' Bruce explains, 'I scheduled a meeting with my local Member of Parliament, to seek his advice.'

'Geoff Wilson? He's my MP, too.'

'He started his career as a barrister and union official before joining the Labor Party. I was sure he would put us in a box, say we're endangering babies.

'I was prepared to argue with him about the evidence and made sure I dressed to look respectable.'

This elicits a giggle from me. His idea of dressing up is brown corduroy pants, a knitted jumper with a hole in the shoulder, worn boots and his sweat-stained Akubra.

'Do you even own a tie?' I can't resist.

'Goodness, no!' Bruce is humouring me. 'I polished my boots.'

'Anyway,' he continues, 'Geoff welcomed me into his office and started the conversation by picking up a photo of his children. Told me they were born at home, one in Sydney and one in Brisbane.

'Geoff was supportive. He became our parliamentary champion in Queensland, only because we couldn't find a sympathetic woman to do it. And guess what?'

I momentarily take my eyes from the road in expectation. 'What?'

'You know Deirdrie Cullen? Behind the calendar fundraiser. *Bellies, Bots, Boobs and Babes?*'

I glance expectantly at Bruce. He's leading up to something. We've been leaving a calendar in every office we visit.

'Geoff called me the other day to advise that the calendar was embarrassing to male MPs.'

'That's ridiculous!' I snort. Beautiful black and white images of pregnant women. Some postnatal and breastfeeding images too. All tasteful. Natural. How many of those men wouldn't balk at a Page 3 bikini girl, or a sexy calendar behind the office door?

I return to what we did today. 'Do you think these women have a chance of being elected?'

'It's not the point,' says Bruce. 'Their candidacy counts for something. They represent the female swing vote for the Gold Coast.'

I deliver Bruce to his bus stop with a promise to be at tomorrow's meeting for some last-minute strategizing.

I'm a consumer representative on a waterbirth policy review committee at the Royal. It's a voluntary role, but I'm excited to sit at the table, even with seven-month-old Kyle in tow. I want to understand how hospital mechanisms work.

We're reviewing the viability of the shallow triangular tubs installed four years ago in every birth suite. The tubs have never been used; banned from the day they cut the ribbon on the Ned Hanlon building. There's a rumour some midwives in the birth suites are happy as they have no interest in conducting waterbirths. But women in labour feel entitled to use them by dint of their very presence.

Co-incidentally, the chair of the working group is the Midwifery Unit Manager who suggested FBC use King George Square for our demonstration. She introduces all the attendees to each other; a mixture of midwives who collectively have conducted hundreds of waterbirths, clinical specialists like obstetricians and neonatologists who admit they have never conducted or even observed any waterbirths, and two consumers, including me.

The other consumer representative, Jan Cornfoot, is a retailer of midwifery books and resources. She has done this sort of thing before. As a complete novice in this setting, I let her take the lead and accept that my job is to ask the stupid questions. The District Manager offers his apologies, again. He's a very busy man.

One obvious benefit of having consumers in the room is that the conversation is dumbed down. Clinicians can't rely upon the jargon of their workaday to explain their decision-making processes. I've never worked in a corporate, or health care environment before. How do you determine that a practice like waterbirth is as safe as pharmacological pain relief? Are any other interventions as safe as water in treating labour fatigue?

The first task was to collate anecdotal evidence and any peer reviewed research that reveals the science of birthing in water – to bring everyone in the room up to date. They survey women's feedback on using water immersion – to rest in the buoyancy of water or give birth. Clinical feedback from midwives and obstetricians comes next.

A young neonatologist gestures my way. 'Lovely to see a happy, healthy, water born baby. We know women want to use water in labour – but how do we know it's risk-free for babies?' He reckons nothing will give us a better snapshot of safety than a review of waterbirth outcomes right here at the Royal.

Karen Marshall, midwife at the Birth Centre – where waterbirths have been conducted for the past nine years – offers to review the Birth Centre data. I happen to already know there have been no adverse outcomes at the Royal. Karen told me so. I'm excited by the possibility that this committee might be able to make a change as significant as this.

The chairwoman declares the meeting closed. She gathers and taps her papers on the desk. Noting my confident smile, she adds, 'Just because no babies have died doesn't mean none ever will.'

My face falls.

'Sometimes, babies die,' she asserts. '1 in 100, at or around their due date. In 20 years, all our technology hasn't improved that number.'

She shakes her head as we parade out of the room, 'Everyone who works in childbirth knows it's not a matter of if, but when.'

22 FORUM FAMILY

Late January 2004

I pick up the remote control and turn on the electronic babysitter. Like moths to a flame, the kids swarm toward it. The volume's too loud, I can plainly hear it from the other room. I feel guilty, but I've made my choice. It gives me personal space and sanity.

Paul's away on a business trip. It's second nature to us now. Usually it takes a day or two to adjust, and then the kids and I find our stride. I'm more disciplined when he's away. I wash the dishes after dinner, get the bin out the night before garbage collection, start dinner early, and go to bed when I'm tired.

I do often feel lonely and pine for adult company. If I didn't have online friendships and the intellectual stimulation of the *Natural Parenting* forum, I'd be a desperately miserable and hollow hausfrau.

I switch on the kettle to make a cup of tea and enjoy a little me time. Some forum members love to debate but I'm not one of them. The heat of conflict disturbs other aspects of my life. But I learn a lot about how others frame their world through the personalities that frequent this online space. A new member has made a strong impression.

After JCF introduces herself as 'Janet Fraser, mother of one, with one on the way,' there's a shift in the group. Her first birth was a traumatic caesarean, and her second baby will be born at home with a private midwife. Many other members of the forum have similar stories and she receives a lot of sympathy from our community.

Gradually though, her presence on the forum is becoming a polarising influence. Feminists love her plain talking, even brutal, honesty. She's witty and smart, but there's a jagged edge. The timid parents who are all about unconditional love and crystal healing have recoiled in horror that a natural parent could incite such venom in 'our safe space'. A typical discussion thread unfolds like this:

Support to VBAC in hospital

Raven: In 2002 my twins were born by caesarean at a local private hospital. I endured a lot of physical pain and separation from my babies in NICU. This time I have a singleton pregnancy and I'm planning a vaginal birth, same doctor, same hospital. Please share all your tips and tricks for a successful VBAC.

Effusive love and support pour forth from members of the forum. Advice like, 'here's what worked for me' and, 'print multiple copies of your birth plan and post one at the door for all to read'.

JCF: Have a homebirth. You'll never get the birth you want in a hospital.

Raven: I'm not comfortable having a homebirth. My husband won't support it either. I like my obstetrician. I'm happy with my choices. I just want my wishes to be respected, to avoid any dramas.

JCF: Bollocks! It's your body, YOUR baby! Husband doesn't get a say in that. You won't get KnOBS and medwives to honour your birth plan. Why not look for an independent midwife to honour your wishes at home?

My fingers drum at the keyboard, but I don't respond. Janet's alternative words for obstetricians and midwives rubs me the wrong way, but they're slowly catching on and other users on the forum are adopting them too. We're supposed to be a gentle parenting community and while the odd swear word slips through now and then, we aren't in the habit of name calling.

> Raven: My OBSTETRICIAN doesn't want to set me up for surgery. We've discussed it at length. I have his support to trial labour. I just know he won't be there for the early stages and I won't have control over which midwives I'll get. Your advice isn't helpful, Janet. In fact, it's hurtful. Thanks anyway.

That could have been the end of the discussion, but it doesn't stop there. Janet is insistent.

> 'Trial' labour? I've never heard of a hospital birth where a woman didn't have to fight for her best chance of a normal vaginal birth. They'll impose intrusions without your consent, because the institution doesn't tolerate women who decline recommended care pathways. And as soon as you stop feeling safe, you stop being safe and so does your baby. You're both fucked if you give birth in hospital.

I get it. It's hard to have an unhindered birth under bright lights with strangers regularly entering the room wanting to touch you, examine you, ask you questions. Performance anxiety is real, and the institutional clock is ticking. Her point is valid. But I have to add my piece:

> Janet, I'm a consumer rep and I hear many happy stories. Not just from the Birth Centre, but the birth suites too. I don't think you can assume that birth plans aren't respected. Midwives and doctors do care about people,

and they care about safety. They don't want to set anyone up for a bad birth. What's in it for them if they do that?

JCF: Jodie Miller, you're a consumer rep? Just another hospital apologist! You know as well as I do how efficiency and convenience and legal concerns come first, how concerns for babies put mothers on the periphery.

Me: You really don't think hospitals can do birth better and kinder? Respect women's choices?

Janet: Just reject the system altogether and have your baby at home. Hospitals will get the message. My caesarean was traumatic. It shouldn't have happened. And afterwards I felt violated, like a kind of rape.

I can't explain why her words sting, but they do. I see my friends and myself as pushing back against the hospital birth machine. Rape is a strong term, but I get it. 'Your pelvis is small,' or 'Your baby is big,' gets dropped on women as early as their first prenatal appointment. In any other context this would be called *grooming*, with a purpose to normalise interventions and discourage women from getting too ambitious about their births. Obstetric violence is real. Some midwives and doctors, consciously or not, exploit the passive and suggestible state of giving birth, performing pre-emptive interventions, perceiving them as consensual when actually, they aren't. If you're a clinician who has seen everything that can go wrong at a birth, how do you stop fear from influencing your practice?

At least, being a consumer rep in my role with Friends of the Birth Centre, I know someone at the Royal is paying attention, reading our newsletters and replying to our letters.

To pile on the stress, all three children have been sick with a flu. We're on the mend but Kyle has developed conjunctivitis. I do my best to perform the impossible and contain the infection naturally, which involves lots of hand washing, laundry, sunshine and sanitising of surfaces. Kyle's eyes don't get better. In fact, after putting him to bed with one slightly bloody eye, I post to my forum friends asking them if I've delayed too long taking my toddler to the doctor.

Motherly support, forgiveness and home remedies pour forth from all over Australia. Breastmilk. Camomile tea. Colloidal silver. Eyebright tea.

I've tried the first two already and I don't possess the third – don't even know what it is. But then forum member, Ceres, offers to drive her jar of eyebright tea out right now so we can have it for treatment first thing in the morning.

We exchange some private messages with my address and phone number. I still don't believe she would do this. I leave my porch light on so she can find my house in the dark. At 9 pm there's a quiet knock on my door. If I've done something crazy, inviting a person from the internet into my home, I feel too desperate to worry about that now.

I open the door. Standing there, I presume, is Ceres – also known as Olivia – with a shock of curly hair, and unexpectedly, her husband and two-year-old daughter. She proffers a glass jar containing brown chaff.

'This is it?'

'This is it.' And we laugh. Strangers no more.

She introduces her husband and daughter, Chelsea, who gravitates to the mess of children's toys on the living room floor. We boil the kettle and I extract a teapot from my cupboard while Olivia explains what to do. She scoops two spoonsful into the pot, 'It's just tea, so make it like tea.'

I pour the hot water, wondering about the dynamic that's emerging between her and the new member, JCF.

'You two seem to have hit it off on the forum.' I watch for her reaction.

'Oh yeah, I totally feel her. We've exchanged a few phone calls. Her sensibilities sit right with my studies in feminism. I know she's upset a few with her comments, but she means well.'

'I can tell. I guess we were all just a little too cosy. It doesn't hurt to shake things up now and then.'

'Indeed.' Olivia pours the pot of amber coloured tea through a coffee filter into my sterile glass jar. 'Let this cool, then apply directly to the eyes as drops, or soak some gauze and use it like a poultice. It's very soothing.'

'Thank you,' I reflexively give her a hug. 'You've done such a thoughtful thing, driving across town at this hour of the night, with your family and all.'

She shakes her curly head. 'Really, it was good for us too. Chelsea was bouncing off the walls. Stan thought it might be good to drive through the night and have a sleeping child when we get home.

The next morning, I follow her instructions to the letter and treat myself and the other children too. By the afternoon I notice a substantial improvement, so I make more tea and continue to apply it as eyedrops to Kyle. The next morning, he's clearly on the mend. Disaster averted – thanks to my new forum friend.

23 A NEW BROOM

February 2004

Polling day is Saturday, February 7 and by Thursday the Beattie Government is declared. Perfect for us, as our work to date would not be wasted and a new Minister for Health will be the cherry on top.

Gordon Nuttall, Member for Sandgate since the early nineties, comes from a background in the trade unions. He was previously Parliamentary Secretary to the Premier, then Minister for Industrial Relations. We hope this means he's primed for the scope and scale of the health portfolio.

Fifty or sixty of us, mostly women, plus babies and children, the usual rent-a-crowd, gather for a rally in the forecourt of the Queensland Health Executive Building on George Street. We now know this rally is redundant, but we have to go through the motions in case the media respond to the press release issued days ago. That would be a bonus.

I have my children, and several other women from Friends of the Birth Centre bring theirs, too. I've dressed the children in their A Midwife Helped Me Out t-shirts. Friends from other networks have come too, their children wearing their organisational shirts. Several midwives are here, too. We're a swarm of rainbow colours, with a predominance of purple, along with all the noise that comes with babies and small children. Passers-by check us out with curiosity.

Prior to the election, Bruce forwarded an email from the office of Premier Beattie offering two things should Labor win the upcoming Queensland election. The first was a monumental 2.3 million dollars for a Birth Centre in the Gold Coast University Hospital upgrade, with funds for other hospitals too, such as the Mater. The second, a pledge that Queensland will immediately conduct a state-wide Maternity Services Review, that all services be officially investigated from small rural hospitals to enormous institutions like the Royal.

The mood in the crowd is jubilant, if a little uncertain, waiting for confirmation of a Birth Centre. We gather in the forecourt for the announcement, waiting patiently to meet our new Minister for Health. Cesca bought a new straw broom as a gimmick for the Minister, supposedly to sweep the portfolio clean from the prior administration. Her press release for *The Courier-Mail* read: *A New Broom For The Health Minister.*

Premier Beattie isn't in attendance, but one of his advisors invites Bruce and Cesca inside to present the broom and talk election promises.

Someone brings a microphone and speaker, and everyone is invited to speak to the crowd. Dr Sarah Buckley talks about the unacceptable caesarean rate, then Jenny Gamble orates on the disempowerment and underutilisation of midwives. Both speak with clarity and conviction, and the crowd is responsive, even without the presence of the media. Bruce returns to take the mic; the news is official. To the sound of applause, he announces the Gold Coast Hospital upgrade will include a Birth Centre. The crowd swallows him up with congratulatory handshakes and hugs.

Anouk emerges from the melee and takes the discarded microphone. I'm transported back to the circle at Windsor House, when she harangued me. I nudge the person next to me asking, 'Shouldn't we stop her?' As if reading my mind, Dr Buckley steps forward and with a maternal nod, takes the microphone away.

As the crowd disperses, Anouk grasps me by the shoulder.

'Hey, I remember you.'

I'm unsure how to respond. Then she breaks into a smile.

'Venus says thanks for the food. She and the baby are doing well.'

Late February 2004

MP Geoff Wilson advised us not to dive deep on an issue until the relationship is established. Don't go in hard at the start. The magic happens later with persistent follow up. This is Bruce's particular talent, but as the campaign gains momentum, we're learning to do it without him. He can't be everywhere at once.

Bruce calls me saying a woman, a client at the Birth Centre, contacted him asking for help.

'She has declined the nineteen-week scan that gives you entry to Birth Centre care. Can you take it on?'

'I'm not sure, Bruce. You could do that in the old Birth Centre, but not now.'

'Exactly. There's no evidence to suggest her pregnancy has complications, and the Royal is a tertiary hospital, for goodness sake. If they can do heart-lung transplants, they can probably manage the birth of a baby without the diagnostic wisdom of an ultrasound. You need to advocate for this woman, Jodie.'

'But...how? Can't you help?'

'I'm up to my eyeballs in appointments so you'll have to go it alone. You're ready.'

'I don't feel ready.'

'Just make an appointment with the Head of Maternity. Then turn up and talk.'

'I've been to enough meetings with you, Bruce, to know it's not that simple.'

'Here's the thing. The woman is entitled to decline the ultrasound. It's called Informed Refusal, and she's done her homework. Sarah Buckley gave me some quotable statistics. Write this down.

'Ultrasound detects fewer than half the major foetal anomalies. 5% of diagnoses may be inaccurate, leading to further scans and tests that come to nothing, causing parents unnecessary worry and, at about $70 per scan, needlessly consuming hospital resources. The midwives in Maternity Outpatients have identified a strong heartbeat, a high placenta, and the mother is healthy in every measurable way. She's declining the ultrasound because, if some structural abnormality indicates there's a genetic condition, she wouldn't terminate or intervene. This mother has decided she doesn't want to play ball with the system. The odds are overwhelmingly in favour of a normal, healthy, uneventful birth. Why shouldn't she use the Birth Centre?'

I make the appointment with the Head of Maternity and prepare myself to debate statistics. I wear my best professional clothes, carrying a clipboard, pen and Paul's old briefcase. I sit opposite the executive and freeze. I look at my notes and read the statistics to a person fully aware of the numbers. She responds that if they let every woman make such a choice, they would be drowning in emergencies. I sense that she's patronising me and I don't blame her. I have no authority here.

A week later Bruce forwards an email from the woman, revealing that the Royal paid to transfer her care to Selangor Private Hospital. I suppose they think it's cheaper than a lawsuit.

The election results have generated a small buzz on the *Natural Parenting* forum, but we quickly revert to our usual chit chat and debate. Rianna, a relatively new member of the forum, has announced her pregnancy. She's a single mum, and she's remaining tight-lipped about who the father is. She does say it's the same father for her firstborn and they planned this pregnancy. How intriguing!

She adds that her first birth was a medically managed induction with epidural. She had a normal vaginal birth but couldn't move or push with her natural urges, which she found undignified. She knows she can give birth, but she's concerned she won't be able to tolerate the pain. Everyone reading the forum responds similarly.

> What you need is a doula. Someone who can advocate for you.

Rianna and I've met a few times at play group, so I feel comfortable making a suggestion.

> What if that advocate was me? I know some of the maternity staff at the Royal and I'm familiar with their policy.

Rianna accepts my offer. We continue to meet regularly throughout her pregnancy and talk about my role. She only wants me to be her mediator with the hospital staff, which I feel qualified to do. Also, it's a little lonely not having a partner to share the journey with. I admire her. She's an independent woman. Self-employed, owns her own home – or at least the mortgage for it.

I confess to her, 'I missed the first birth I was meant to attend.' It feels important to be transparent.

'If things happen so fast that you can't make it, what a wonderful bonus. But if things don't follow the expected path, I might need you on my team.'

'I can do that, Rianna. It would be my honour.'

A few weeks later, I receive a letter from the Royal inviting me to participate in a working group drafting policy for health consumer engagement. And another to establish 'alternative care pathways' for maternity services. Could this mean the hospital is making internal plans to consult and accommodate choices? The first one is paid. The second one, unpaid, and as usual they're on different days. I'm out of pocket for childcare, but the chair of the working group concedes to at least waive my parking.

24 HOLDING OUT FOR A GRANT

March 2004

Friends of the Birth Centre now represents around 300 Brisbane families, and we're being monitored by the Royal, plus several advocacy groups. New members with skills are stepping up and our committee is invigorated by the influx.

We've been scheduling meetings fortnightly, becoming weekly in the lead up to version two of Airing Our Laundry, on the first of May. Event plans are simmering nicely.

Melissa Fox, who joined us when she was researching her birth options, delighted us by announcing her pregnancy. She's a boon, using her contacts in film and TV to coordinate all the media.

We've applied for a grant. If we don't get the $6000, our vision of matching white marquees and a stage is at stake. Fortunately, we've locked in sponsorship deals with Aromababy and Brisbane Sound, and Hills Australia have, thankfully, agreed to lend us their rotary clothes hoists again. The show will go on. All the community groups receive a free stall. Businesses selling or promoting baby goods, massage, yoga, well-being, and natural cleaning have bought the bulk of the commercial stalls, making the event viable if we get the grant for the marquees.

Our secretary, Emma, has engaged Brisbane radio personality, Robin Bailey, as our spokesperson. Robin's second child was born at the Birth Centre. Kareena's husband Brendan, of Australian Acting Academy, will have his student performers roam the crowd. Brisbane blues artist, Barbara Fordham, will perform just days before her due date, and we're selfishly hoping she doesn't go early.

Caroline McCullough is running the stage program, even though, as a double caesarean mother, she'll never use the Birth Centre. She'll perform an original song she wrote for the occasion.

There'll be two panel discussions in the breaks on stage. And there'll be activities like baby massage workshops, and toddler sing-alongs. For adults, there'll be a presentation on acupuncture and Chinese herbs in pregnancy. Birthtalk will facilitate A Letter To My Midwife, giving women a chance to debrief about their births and give feedback to their hospitals. The agenda is full.

All the while, there are our regular obligations, like the New Mothers' Morning Teas. We need our fundraisers like the Baby Goods Sale and the hospital Baked Goods Sale because if we don't get the grant, we'll be drawing every laboriously earned dollar from FBC's bank account.

No one has complained about having too much to do. While our agenda highlights the long waiting list for the Birth Centre, the unified message of all the advocacy groups is 'choice in childbirth'. It feels important, and with a Birth Centre in the works for the Gold Coast, we feel an obligation to keep the conversation going.

I meet Rianna in the foyer of the Ned Hanlon Building. As her support person, I'm joining her tour of the birthing suites. Having only really known the Birth Centre, I'm eager to see the other side of maternity at the Royal.

Our guide is a middle-aged woman lacking much warmth. She shows us around one of the birthing suites currently not in use, with a warming cupboard for heat packs, towels and sheets, and a state-of-the-art, height-adjustable, hospital bed with detachable stirrups; a feature we're supposed to coo about.

The triangular tub in the corner stirs questions from one of the women.

'Can we use the tub?'

'I'm sorry to say you can't. It's being reviewed by the hospital, but there's a shower and toilet in every suite.'

I don't say anything about my role in the review.

'I don't understand,' the woman becomes insistent. 'Why can't we use the tub? Not to give birth. Just to rest? Soak a bit?'

'I'm sorry to say, there are no plugs. You can't soak. You can't use the tub at all.'

'What if I bring my own plug?'

I can't hide my smile.

The midwife has the final word, redirecting us to the reclining chair and the fit ball in one corner of the room. I see no bean bags or pull out mattresses for getting comfortable on the floor. No birth stools either. I know they get borrowed from the Birth Centre all the time. Equipment that FBC fundraised to buy.

No one explains about the foetal heart monitor that's strapped to your belly for the first 20 minutes after you arrive, and for much of your labour if you opt for an epidural. Nor do they show us the electrode they screw into the baby's skull to monitor vital signs during a protracted second stage. The stirrups are not installed on the bed at this moment. The room lacks the family-centred comforts of the Birth Centre, but it's adequate. This is Queensland Health. What are we expecting? A hipster hotel suite?

For her wedding anniversary, I lend Caroline my favourite cookbook of seduction: Intercourses, An Aphrodisiac Cookbook. How could I have known I'd be complicit in the surprise conception of another baby? Third time lucky. Despite two prior caesareans, she wastes no time preparing herself for birth.

25 AOL2

May 2004

We collectively exhale. Friends of the Birth Centre got the grant for the marquees and stage. The committee is invigorated knowing we'll be able to stage our vision.

The only available day we could hire King George Square clashes with the flights Paul and I bought for a New Zealand family holiday. We agree to postpone. This event can't happen any other time and New Zealand isn't going anywhere.

Like last time, I pack the car the night before. FBC has struggled to obtain as many baby clothes this time, but if we hang the clothes a little more sparsely, no one will know the difference.

I arrive to marquees, stage and sound, already in position. The team and I step back. 'Look what we did!' We allow ourselves a moment to take it all in.

This time, Paul is home and able to bring the children in later for the fun. The guys turn up at 6 am to position the bases. There's a lot to do, so I rally early arrivals towards the bags of baby clothes with instructions for how to hang them to best effect.

Three midwives from Maternity Coalition wear the Suffragette costumes and carry the *Choice In Birth* placards from the Labor Women's dinner. The audience gives their attention to panel discussions, followed by pantomime, children's activities, and parachute games. When I circle back to check on the clothes lines, I see pegging the baby clothes has been abandoned. It's disappointing, particularly in light of our sponsorship arrangement, but we're already halfway through the day and it's too late to fix it now.

I'm largely relieved of responsibility, taking Emma's advice to guide the media to Robin Bailey and any attending mothers with bellies and babes. They present a more powerful image than I ever could. I mingle and strike up conversations with the public and our wonderful, supportive stall holders. The incidental crowd are curious, and sympathetic. It's amazing who will tell you their story, if you only take a moment to ask.

At the end of the day Bruce's wife, Erika, who recently announced her pregnancy, catches me by the arm to tell me what a fine day she's had and how proud she is of our achievement.

'This,' she says, 'is what a small group of passionate people can do.'

'You're part of it, too,' I say, pushing down my disappointment over the clotheslines. There was a synergy today between the groups that can only be good for our future work together.

'I watched the people talking to Bruce,' she says. 'They all know who he is. My humble man is actually rather important.'

'We wouldn't have this crowd without him,' I confirm.

She smiles, radiant. 'And I get to take him home.'

We giggle at that. I know what she's saying. So many of the women in my circle have experienced tension in their homes because their husbands weren't supportive. Paul is the enabler for my community work, like Erika is for Bruce.

Driving home, Paul receives a notification. It's time to board our flight to Auckland.

'Didn't you cancel the tickets?' he asks.

'No, I thought you did!'

Money wasted. It could have flared into an argument, but what's the point? We simmer in silence all the way home. It's a total spoiler, but we have to let it go.

Financially, FBC broke even by selling our merchandise. We didn't have to dip into our lifeboat fund, which is an enormous relief. We achieved our goal and presented a united front for maternity reform. Everyone was pleased. Or so I thought.

The next day, the FBC committee meet at a coffee shop in Windsor to debrief. I'm fifteen minutes late, and as I take a seat the conversation stops, and everyone looks at me.

'What's up?' I ask. Hannah is playing with her cheesecake, refusing eye contact.

Emma answers. 'What was all that yesterday? The pantomime. The people in costume with placards. That's not us. Who were they?'

I rock back in my chair. 'I told you Maternity Coalition would be there. We gave them a stall, right Kath?' She nods half-heartedly.

'You didn't say they would walk around in costume with placards. It was uncomfortable.'

Kath is nodding in agreement. I don't understand. I thought we conveyed the right message. Hannah is still stabbing her cheesecake. She knew that all the birth groups would be there.

'You know I'm the Secretary of Maternity Coalition. I've been working with them for a year now.'

'I knew you were liaising with them,' Emma retorts, 'but Secretary? That's news.'

'They needed someone to take minutes. It's informal. Not a big deal.'

'It's a big deal if you don't tell us. And a conflict of interest.'

'How? We all want the same thing!'

'I don't want a homebirth, Jodie. I want to support the Birth Centre and elevate the midwives, not associate with those radicals. If that's us, I quit!'

I only drink half my hot chocolate, skip the cake, and go home to soak a box of Kleenex. What did I do wrong? There are only two Birth Centres in Queensland. What option does everyone else have? I feel caught in the gap between 'have' and 'have not'. Can't they see the big picture?

26 BORN BEFORE ARRIVAL

June 2004

The annual Parents, Babies and Children's Expo is the single biggest opportunity for us to promote the Birth Centre. It's a popular gig for new members, so we're rarely short of volunteers. We beg a raffle prize from our newsletter advertisers and the sale of the tickets, plus our merchandise, covers the cost of the stall.

Representing FBC at the Expo is one of my favourite things to do. Women who approach us come from one of two camps. Either they know the Birth Centre, maybe even had a baby there – or would have if they could. These women stop to have a chat, share their birth stories and introduce their little ones. The second camp hasn't heard of the Birth Centre and doesn't understand the model of care. They've already subscribed to private health insurance and taken the private-hospital, private-obstetrician route, believing it to be gold standard maternity care. Only a few will have researched that choice.

A pregnant woman approaches me at the stand, along with two non-pregnant friends. She cradles a milkshake in one hand and her round belly with the other. I estimate she's about six months into her first pregnancy and naturally anxious about the inevitability of giving birth. I remember feeling like that too.

'I'm booked into North West Private Hospital,' she says, 'with a lovely obstetrician. I'd really like a natural birth. How do I make that happen?'

I blink. It takes me a moment to digest her question. Two midwives from North West Private approached me earlier pouring love upon the Birth Centre and its low caesarean rate. They said their hospital was well over 40%, with a majority induction and epidural rates too. Not that the hospital, or the individual doctors, are obliged to reveal that. I know beautiful, natural births happen there, but mostly for experienced mothers who've given birth before.

I want to say, *leave your obstetrician*, but that isn't helpful.

'Well,' I shrug, 'have you had this conversation with your care provider?'

'What conversation?'

'That you want a natural birth. Have you told your doctor?'

'Oh, he says it's too early for that.'

'Well,' I begin, 'there are lots of ways to hone your instincts. Have you heard of YogaBaby?'

'I hate yoga,' she replies.

'It's more than that. It's childbirth education too, and a way to meet other mothers.'

'Nah-ah, not my scene.'

'Okay,' I continue, 'would you consider hiring a doula?'

'A doo-la. What's that?' She looks at her girlfriends and they laugh.

'A person who's your companion and advocate. Birth support. Evidence shows you have a better chance of a spontaneous vaginal birth with a doula.'

'My husband wants to do that.'

'Has your husband given birth before?' I snap, then cough. 'A doula can support your husband too.'

'No, I mean, what can I do to be ready for birth. I don't want a caesarean. My sister had one, and it was awful.'

'Ah, I see.' I know this story too well. How much do you say to a woman on the slippery slope to a cascade of interventions she doesn't want? She's asking for easy answers that tick her boxes, and that's not how it works.

I muster all the empathy I can and lean in, conspiratorially. She mirrors me and leans in as well. Her girlfriends cock their ears in my direction, not wanting to miss something juicy.

'Think about this,' I say in a low voice. 'How did the baby get in there?' I check they're following. They lean in closer, listening, eyes sparkling.

'We're mammals. A physiological birth needs the same conditions to let the baby out as it did to let baby in. Think about what you want when you're making love. You want privacy, dim lights, connection with your partner. You need to feel safe. Unobserved. Birth flows when you release the same hormones as love making. Think loving thoughts, move like you're making love, play music that feels sexy.'

The women blush and I worry that I've crossed a line.

'Finally,' I lean back and try to look professional, 'staying home as long as you can before going to the hospital gives you the best chance of avoiding interventions.'

'But what about the pain?' she asks with fear in her eyes.

I touch her arm. 'I can't tell you it won't hurt, but it's not pain like an injury. It's pain with a purpose.' She looks at me like maybe she's beginning to understand. 'Pain is communication. It tells you to move and find more comfortable positions that will let the baby out. If labour starts naturally, and you can move freely to manage your discomfort, your brain will release endorphins that soften the worst of it. I promise.'

'How many babies have you had?' she asks, testing my authority.

'Three. No epidural. No pethidine. Not even a graze to my perineum. Learn as much as you can while you have time. Let labour start naturally, if you can.'

The three women step back. They've heard enough. They walk away deep in conversation, but I can't tell whether my oversharing was helpful or not. And the hardest thing is, I'll never know how her baby's birth will be for her. Statistically, I know the odds aren't in her favour.

September 2004

I open *The Courier-Mail* to the health section. An article by IVF doctor, David Molloy, Queensland President of the Australian Medical Association, has leapt from *The Australia and New Zealand Journal of Obstetrics and Gynaecology Vol 6, No 3*, to the editorial section of *The Courier-Mail*.

Caesarean sections a legitimate choice

And the by-line: *Reproductive freedom for women includes choosing how they'll give birth, argues David Molloy.*

Maternity Coalition is all about choice informed by evidence. What we find though is often a push back from women who are confronted. 'My caesarean was an emergency' (it might have been). 'My epidural was necessary' (sometimes it is). But all the available evidence suggests that messing with nature's design has consequences. With vaginal birth, babies receive the gift of their mother's microbiome, inoculating their immune systems and, we now know, offering better health outcomes for life. Mothers also benefit. We're hormonally primed for bonding and breastfeeding. If prevention is the future of maternity care, woman-centred, health-focussed, models of care make logical and economic sense. Funding that follows the woman, reducing the bloat of unnecessary or unwanted procedures, also makes sense. But how do we even begin to change it?

The AMA is a formidable medico-political opponent with the unquestioned respect of the public. Rumoured to have a personal caesarean rate of 50%, does Dr Molloy's advocacy for surgical birth suggest Maternity Coalition is making headway with our campaign for better birth choices? I hope so. Ultimately, the AMA is a doctors' union, formed to protect the reputation, and income, of the medical profession. Evidence informs opinion, surely. *The Hippocratic Oath* and *the Declaration of Geneva* have fallen out of favour, but the modus operandi still recognises patient autonomy and dignity, and the importance of well-being. Their primary obligation is to patients first, before colleagues and society.

First, do no harm.

July 2004

Rianna continues to juggle self-employment and caring for her four-year-old son. The last time I saw her I brought a batch of ravioli in a veg-loaded Napoli sauce, for quick and easy meals when the baby is born. She plans to work until she goes into labour and return as soon as she feels able. Self-employment means there's no maternity leave. On the day contractions begin I'm with Paul and the children on our land beyond Brisbane, with limited mobile phone service.

I discover Rianna's missed call and return it immediately. She says her contractions are starting to bite.

'Shall I come now?'

'Not yet. There's plenty of time. My friend, Louise, is here.'

'You're the boss. Just give me plenty of notice.' I already explained I'm fifty minutes from the hospital, via home to drop off Paul and the kids, and it'll take another fifteen minutes to park and find Rianna in the birth suites.

Remembering my experience with Rose, I load the car and get the children ready. Best we leave now. Paul can drive.

Twenty minutes later, as we near our street, my mobile phone rings. This time, it's Louise.

'Jodie, I think you should come now.'

'We're almost home. Won't take long. Meet you at the hospital.'

'Ah, about that. Rianna can't talk through contractions. We spent the afternoon downloading stopwatch programs, you know, for timing them. Then, Rianna asked me to go to the bottle shop, for some bubbles to celebrate later. I'm back and now she says she wants to push.'

She wants to push. What were they thinking?

'Shit! Call an ambulance!' Paul looks at me with alarm.

'We have,' Louise assures me.

'We're coming straight to you.' I gesture at Paul to keep driving. We'll have to skip our detour home. There won't be time for that now.

All we can do is drive at the speed limit, all the way to Rianna's house. The traffic crawls. We round the corner behind the sirens, and yes, they lead to her driveway. I bound out of the car and sprint up the hill to her door, up the stairs to the room where I can hear a bustle of people, then the reassuring cry of a newborn. I enter to a puddle of baby on the bed, still attached to Rianna, who's leaning back on a pile of pillows, a surprised expression on her face. She looks like a woman who's just had delightful, vigorous sex. She didn't need my support. That much is apparent.

The ambulance attendants seem reluctant to touch the baby more than necessary. They wrap him in a warm towel and, leaving the umbilical cord attached, hand him to Rianna for cuddles. She looks very pleased with herself and clearly adores her baby.

A few minutes later, she says she's uncomfortable and wants to push again, but the officers advise it would be better if they took the ambulance to deliver the placenta in the Emergency Department. Do they think she should just hold it in?

Rianna needs to push now. The emergency worker cuts the cord and hands the baby to Louise. I rummage around in Rianna's kitchen and find my ravioli container, which I place into her toilet in time for her to sit and release the placenta. I pop the lid on, relieved that everything seems to have gone very well.

The ambulance driver gets Rianna's consent to take her to hospital. They aren't interested in the placenta at all, but I hand over the container, anyway. Midwives at the Birth Centre always inspected my placenta after birth, checking for completeness, with no tissue retained that might later become septic. Tamara had demonstrated how all the parts fit together, respectfully lifting the organ, from inside the sac, over the back of her hand.

She'd said, 'Imagine baby is upside down, his bottom in the palm of my hand.' She used her other hand to draw the tissue up, pointing with a spare finger. 'Here's how the membranes encased your baby and where the placenta attached to your uterus. Check out the system of blood vessels that converge at the umbilicus.' This wonderful, life-growing, organ never receives any credit. Irreverently disposed of as human waste in the hospital incinerators, its miraculous work goes unacknowledged.

I ride up front with the driver. He opens the window between the cabin and the rear where the other officer rides with Rianna and her baby. We talk about how nice it must be to attend a birth, instead of accidents and acute health emergencies. At the hospital, they unload Rianna on the gurney, and there's the container of placenta on the floor of the ambulance – left behind again. I pick it up and follow wherever they're taking Rianna in a surreal procession through the bowels of the Royal's emergency rooms. They check her into maternity, and we proceed to the wards where Rianna is allocated a bed.

A midwife enters and automatically closes the privacy curtain saying, 'Let's have a little look at what's going on down there.' She doesn't introduce herself or check Rianna's name. She just dips under the sheet and asks her to spread her knees.

'You have a tiny tear there. We'll arrange to get that stitched for you.'

I step in. 'Rianna, do you consent?' The midwife gives me the side eye. I'm not opposed to stitches, just the impersonal way she's going about her job. Shouldn't there be some sort of introduction before you go poking at a woman's vagina?

'I would recommend she have it stitched,' she asserts and, picking up the ward phone, she orders the procedure. 'Good news, they can fit you in right away.'

Rianna is still high on endorphins, and I get the vibe that if the midwife handed her a ukulele and requested *Tiptoe Through The Tulips*, the new mother would have provided a rousing rendition.

As the wardens wheel her bed to the surgical unit, I approach the nurses' station. 'This is Rianna's placenta,' I say and hand over the container, assuming there's a protocol for dealing with it. The attending nurse takes it with a quizzical look, and I walk away.

Two weeks later, I visit Rianna at home and stash more ravioli in her fridge. She has a temperature of 39 degrees and an appointment with her GP.

A few days later, she emails that she and the baby re-admitted to hospital for a dilation and curettage procedure, or D&C, to remove some retained placenta. We can't always know such things, but maybe it would have been discovered earlier if the placenta had been checked?

As Caroline's belly grows, so does our friendship. We talk as much about day-to-day stuff as we do about birth reform. We discuss our children, and our complicated mothers. We talk about our husbands – both work in IT. We talk recipes and music and our lack of enthusiasm for housework.

Naturally, this baby's birth is a big deal for Caroline. She's experiencing a lot of anxiety, with lingering post-traumatic stress from her previous caesareans. Debbie from Birthtalk, the support group, said she needs to 'walk calm'. I can see that a good birth will jump-start her healing. It'll mean liberation from grief and guilt over past decisions.

'Will you be my labour support, Jodie?'

My heart leaps and tears brim my eyes. 'Caroline,' I declare, 'what an honour!'

Then my heart falls. What if I let her down like I did the other women? I don't have a sparkling track record as a doula and she knows it.

'That's not going to happen again,' she says. 'Just promise me, when I'm in labour, you won't say, 'You can do it!' It sounds patronising.'

'Say, 'You're *doing* it.' It'll help me stay present in the moment.'

I promise I will and love that she asked me to say it.

27 WATERBIRTH

July 2004

A rumour is rippling through FBC, origin unknown, that a baby has died at the Birth Centre. Privacy dictates that details remain confidential while a coronial inquest takes place. I feel very sad for the family and their loss. How devastating to arrive at the Birth Centre in labour and leave without a baby.

I feel for the midwife too, given I know them all so well. Whomever she is, Queensland Health will have suspended her from work. An accident at a birth can change a clinician's practice forever. Midwives must be fearless, to protect the confidence of a mother, yet be vigilant enough to intervene if circumstances necessitate.

The loss of a baby is a terrible tragedy. But losing a mother is worse.

The documentary, *BirthRites*, was on SBS last night. Australia's entire birth network tuned in, and today *Ozmidwifery* is alight with talk about it. Here is the *National Maternity Action Plan* in practice, in a remote territory of Canada, providing culturally sensitive maternity care to Indigenous families with complicated health and social concerns. It demonstrates there's a solution to Australia's dilemma for Indigenous health and Birthing On Country – giving birth on ancestral land so that the child receives spiritual connection to kin and country.

It taps into national momentum towards better birth choices – for everyone, especially the vulnerable in our communities, not just healthy, white, educated women who are asking for Birth Centres and homebirth.

The promised Maternity Services Review launched this month in Queensland. Every community group and government service in this space is invited to prepare a submission. Melissa Fox and I assume responsibility, writing for Friends of the Birth Centre. Bruce and the Maternity Coalition team have the bigger job – to compile and summarise the multitude of letters and emails received in the past three years.

I read an email with a familiar name attached. Philippa Scott lives in Townsville. She's a doula, pregnant with her second baby and she's frustrated by the birth options in her region. Since Premier Beattie gave a Birth Centre to the Gold Coast, she wants one for Townsville too. She's provided her phone number, so I call.

'Call me Pippa,' she says. 'I moved away from my family to Townsville last year, with my husband and our two-month-old baby.'

I suck in my breath, remembering my own early motherhood. Philippa turned to an online parenting forum, *BubHub* – virtual communities are the new 'neighbourhood' – and formed her own local mothers' group. 'I recruited people in parent rooms in shopping centres, everywhere,' she laughs.

When she discovered Maternity Coalition, she'd asked Bruce to connect her with someone local, to debrief about her baby's birth. He'd recommended a local pregnancy yoga teacher who helped her unravel the, unfortunately common, story of how her baby's caesarean birth came to be.

I tell Pip what I know about the Brisbane Birth Centre. The story goes that the closure of Boothville, the Salvation Army's maternity hospital for unmarried mothers, triggered demand for a new birthing service that was equally low intervention. Two idealistic midwives and a supportive registrar managed to get the Birth Centre commissioned in a meeting at the Royal Women's Hospital because, on that day in 1994, their opponent failed to attend.

The midwife-duo, Marg and Karen, operated it as a 'standalone' service in the private wing of the Women's Hospital until the Birth Centre became so popular they were given a third room and later, a dedicated birth tub, where my Elijah was born.

'There was briefly a Birth Centre in Townsville,' I explain, 'that was shut down years ago. At the time, consumer advocacy groups weren't a thing.'

'Should I form a Friends of the Birth Centre in Townsville?' she asks.

'If you're happy to do it,' I say, delighted. 'But in every other regard, don't do what we've done. Townsville can do better.'

'Just you watch me!'

Next thing, she's showing me a sparkly new logo and forwarding minutes from their inaugural meeting.

Mid-September 2004

Paul comes home from work with a bottle of wine.

'You look like you had a good day,' he says.

'We did. Play group this morning, then lunch with Bruce and Erika, then a nap for all three on the way home. Kyle is still sleeping. Maybe for the long haul.'

Paul places the wine on the kitchen bench. He extends his hand and I take it, tangling our fingers like when we first met.

I lead him quietly up the hall and show him the blanket fort between two chairs, a torchlight underneath. Three-year-old Elijah and two-year-old Ruby chatter to each other in their own language, giggling.

'Come on,' Paul winks. 'I'll pour you a glass and rub your feet.'

I draw two dusty glasses from the back of the cupboard.

'It's so different now,' he says as he opens the bottle. 'You seem happier.'

'We had a great day.'

'I mean, all the time. Remember how you used to call me in the afternoons?'

I try not to. I came through my matrescence, stronger now than I ever thought.

'I have friends,' I give Paul a playful push. 'You're not the only one I call.'

He pours and I sip the wine. Nothing can spoil this moment.

'You get satisfaction from doing advocacy?' he says.

'I feel like I've found something I'm good at.'

'Maternity Coalition stuff or mothering stuff?'

'Both I guess.' I pause and consider what I want to say. 'Hannah and Kathy both announced they're pregnant last week.'

'More babies for FBC. That's nice, and...?'

'Well...are we done having babies?'

Paul's face lights up with a smile. He's the youngest of four, himself. We let the silence keep us warm for a few beats. Then, from the back room, Kyle stirs.

I put down my glass. 'There goes my foot rub!'

I shrug. Yes, I've come a long way.

Late September 2004

The waterbirth review at the Royal is all wrapped up with our unanimous vote to trial the banned tubs in the birth suites for pain relief, and to roll out waterbirth accreditation to all interested midwives. District Manager, Dr Richard Olley, hasn't attended a single meeting, but will review the literature and take our submission to the Health Service Board.

One week later, *The Courier-Mail* runs an article, the same day Dr Olley sends the email notifying us that the Royal will not be trialling water immersion outside of the Birth Centre. Occupational Health and Safety deems the tubs too shallow. Under direction from the executive, Dr Olley reinstates the ban on the tubs until a Randomised Control Trial confirms their absolute safety.

Everyone knows, for ethical reasons, a Randomised Control Trial will never be approved. As Bruce likes to say, if you have a number of cars and, regardless of engine, randomly put petroleum in half, and distillate in half, there will be predictable failures. My phone runs hot. There's a flurry of emails. It's a turnaround so surprising I take it personally. Was the whole process a case of smoke and mirrors – an appearance of doing something when the conclusion was predetermined?

I feel like I've flushed family money down the toilet – some six or seven hundred dollars in parking and childcare that we personally absorbed so I could represent women wanting a warm bath instead of an epidural. It seems ridiculous that it's too great a risk for even a trial. What are they going to do now? Remove the tubs?

There will be a protest and it's not just an FBC event. Maternity Coalition and Home Midwifery Association advocates are contributing too.

The women inflate a kiddie pool in the early hours of a cool September morning and carry it up Charlotte Street to the entrance of Queensland Health. Melissa, the leader of the new belly brigade, steps into the empty pool wearing a maternity swimsuit and sits down in solidarity with Erika, due next month, and Caroline, due in January, along with the pregnant owner of the kiddie pool, Sharon Heilbronn.

Dozens of women attend with their children. They hold placards saying *We Won't Take This Lying Down*, and *Water Costs Less Than Drugs*, and *Birth Pools – Women's Choice*. The media arrives to a spectacle. The protest is on the evening news on three stations and gets a half page photo and story in *The Courier-Mail.*

But I'm on the other side of the globe in Ireland with Paul, his mother, and our three little ones, supporting Paul's keynote speech at a conference in Limerick. I follow the action from afar. To date, it's the most visible united front for birth reform in Australia. And I wasn't there to witness it.

November 2004

It's hot the day Bruce and I drive to Toowoomba on the Darling Downs, an hour and a half from Brisbane. We're to meet with midwife, Liz Wilkes, and visit her prototype birth service, Indigo Place. Here, she unapologetically provides independent, caseload, antenatal care. Currently, she's flying under the radar in the conservative regional city.

We greet Liz and her crew of supporters, new mothers and babies, enough people to line the walls of what would once have been the living room in the unassuming, blue-painted suburban house. Bruce presents his digital presentation about Maternity Coalition for the group, who are forming their own Darling Downs chapter. He summarises the *National Maternity Action Plan* and answers their enthusiastic questions. Liz then takes us on a tour to see, firsthand, the alternative service she created. I'm in awe of the bravado of this Australian midwife, returned from working in the UK and frustrated by the dearth of options in her hometown. She's going to change the world.

Melissa Fox gives birth to a daughter, under an experimental, hybrid, model of care. Instead of a caseload midwife, she has a young and progressive female obstetrician who's attempting to build a bridge with the Birth Centre. After more than an hour of pushing, the two women discussed their options. It's surely oppressive, being a young feminist doctor under the conservative scrutiny of the Royal. If anything goes wrong, she might lose credibility and the hospital will bury her project.

Melissa consented to a ventouse delivery. Her baby was born without incident. We can't know for sure, but she wondered if, given more time, she could have given birth under her own steam. Providing an environment for birth isn't just about access to technology and clinical expertise. It's also about people having evidence-based information, to make decisions that are right for them. And it demands that someone with great trust in birth, patiently and lovingly hold the space, giving a mother every chance to say, 'I did it myself.'

28 VBA2C

January 2005

Caroline knows she'll go past 42 weeks, but this time she's willing to wait.

She monitors the baby's movements several times a day. She researches every conceivable complication and discusses it in depth with her midwife at Selangor Private Hospital. It's nearly a two-hour drive from where she lives, but it's the only hospital offering a vaginal waterbirth after two caesareans. I'm still excited to be her doula.

At the end of week 43, Caroline calls me. She and her husband Steven have taken a family holiday and gone up-coast to a resort near the hospital to wait it out. She's having contractions that are increasingly uncomfortable. She thinks she might have a baby today! Being a Saturday, I convince Paul we should pack for a day at the beach and meet her there.

When we arrive, Caroline is having gentle, regular contractions. We settle the kids and dads in for some sand play in the shade while Caroline and I take a walk around the lake. We talk about things like beliefs and trust and feeling safe.

'I've thought long and hard about it,' she says, 'and it was like, the more they pushed me to bring the baby on, the tighter my body became.

'It was like I didn't matter. My sense of what was happening inside my own body didn't matter.'

Hospitals are like a huge machine with multiple moving parts. Everything needs to happen a set way, or the process breaks down. Its why midwives call women clients, not patients. It signals they're in charge. Not the machine.

'Is it too soon to say, 'You're doing it'?'

'Maybe,' she rubs her tummy on the underside, 'but thanks for remembering.'

We continue in silence, taking time to digest the importance of what's happening. The ducks on the lake swarm to a family on the shore throwing bread. We can see our children playing in the sand not far away. Paul looks up and waves.

'Before we join them,' I confide, 'I want to tell you something.' Caroline stops walking and looks at me, cheeks flushed, a glisten of sweat on her brow.

'You know that Paul and I are trying for another baby, right?'

'Oh yes!'

'I might be pregnant. My period's late.'

She releases a tiny squeal and hugs me over her ample belly.

After the walk we get some lunch, but her contractions have petered out. Paul leans in and whispers with annoyance.

'She obviously isn't having a baby today. We should take the kids home. They need to sleep.'

'Not yet,' I hiss. 'We just need to be sure.'

We take the kids for a swim, but the water's cold and really, they're too tired now. We decide that I should stay and catch the train home later if contractions don't pick up. I wave as Paul drives the children away and walk back inside to Steven and Caroline.

There's tension between them. Steven's asking, 'What do we do next?' This is their last night at the resort. Tomorrow they must go home again, away from the hospital and with no childcare for the boys. They spent their budget to be here, waiting things out.

Caroline is overtired, 'Exactly what can I do about that Steven? I can't make this happen at will.' She rubs her stomach where the baby's moving. Her discomfort is obvious.

'What if you took some castor oil?' I say, then regret it. Caroline rolls her eyes. Everyone's rushing her. She decides to take a long walk by herself and call her midwife to talk it out. When she returns, she declares she can wait a bit longer.

The afternoon and evening pass slowly. Steven puts the boys to bed. We order Caroline to run a bath. Steven and I buy takeaway dinner and a bottle of wine. We eat together in their room with stilted conversation. The wine helps us relax and we encourage Caroline to have a half glass in the hope she'll achieve some sleep. She has not had a contraction for many hours now. I ask the couple to tell me how they met, knowing that Caroline just needs to feel safe and loved.

Around 11 pm, Steven drives me to catch the last Brisbane train. It's a two-hour ride home and it has been a long day.

The next morning, I try my best to nap with the children so I can be fresh to drive later, if needed. When I go to the toilet, my period has begun. Bummer.

Around 7.30 pm Steven calls. He's in the car, driving back up the coast. He explains that Caroline checked herself into the hospital this morning, directly from the resort. She's spent the day there in prodromal labour with weak, but regular, contractions; getting her body ready, and the baby positioned for birth.

'Jodie, I know yesterday was a big day, but if you can make it at all, Caroline would like you to be there.'

'Of course,' I say with a nod to Paul, 'We're just putting the kids to bed.'

Within a half hour I'm on my way, driving back to the Sunshine Coast. Steven and I arrive in the car park simultaneously. The night air is humid from summer storms. I wait outside while Steven goes in. Caroline just got out of the bath; her hair is wet. She's rocking slowly on a fitball, fully dressed. She's crying with exhaustion. They embrace and exchange some tender words. Steven goes off to their double room to sleep until Caroline asks for him later.

I go in next and give Caroline a hug. She tells me she's tired and emotional, but glad to see me. Her contractions are regular and painful.

I offer to give her a massage and she thinks that's a great idea. The lights are low, and the room is warm. I find some oil in a drawer and massage her back and shoulders slowly and deeply. Some of the tension begins to slip away.

But I can sense her resistance and suggest she try hanging for a few contractions. It always worked for me. This room isn't set up for weight bearing. Even the door jamb is too high to allow her to dangle by her fingertips and take the pressure off her legs. I offer a chair for support as I roll and wobble her thighs between my palms. She likes this, so I continue for several more contractions, now coming closer together, and then her low moan becomes an ascending 'ahhhhh' and suddenly her midwives, Lynne and Vicki, are at the door.

Lynne reminds Caroline to visit the toilet. Audible behind the door, she's having some whopper contractions. Vicki asks Caroline if she's feeling ready to come out.

'No,' comes Caroline's meek reply, but she lets Vicki in for a pep talk.

Whatever Vicki said hit the spot, and Caroline comes out to try a few new moves. Vicki shows her how to hula, bounce and rock. Lynne raises the bed and rail to full height for Caroline to lean on. If only I had known that earlier! The dancing and bouncing are helping Caroline find her groove. Soon she's naked under a hot shower, singing and cheering herself on, while Lynne fills the large triangular tub in anticipation. I could be wrong, but it looks identical to the tubs denied use in the birth suites at the Royal.

Caroline stomps under the running water and pronounces, 'Yes,' as she talks herself through the contractions. She's loosening up and releasing the sexual energy that's the hallmark of a beautiful, unhindered birth. Her eyes are bright, her cheeks flushed, her pupils dilated, and her movements smooth and intuitive.

The tub is full and Lynne urges Caroline to climb in. Once immersed in the water, her contractions slow down, giving her a chance to rest. For several minutes she sleeps between contractions, exhausted from the tension and friction leading to this night. But soon her labour re-engages, and contractions begin anew. Typical of singers, her birth song echoes through the hallways. Vicki closes some doors and we lament the absence of suitable soundproofing.

It's now 3.30 am and she has been labouring all night. Her contractions change gear, coming wave upon wave, and Caroline asks for Steven. So, I find his guest room in the hospital and wake him from a deep sleep.

Steven and I take turns pressing the dimples of Caroline's lower back during the bitey contractions. She can't talk, merely grunt and nod, and we all read it as a good sign.

With each contraction her voice gets a little shriller. I worry she'll be hoarse tomorrow and she hasn't even begun to push. She's tired. We all are. But I know Caroline's tiredness in my bones. The numbness, the zoned-out other-worldness. It's where she needs to be.

With the next surge Caroline's shrill becomes a scream. Thinking it might help, I do a deep moan and apply the soothing sacral pressure behind her hips. I'm getting excited. Contractions are coming one after the other. There's a red stripe running down the crack of her bottom and debris in the water shows progress is happening.

'You're doing it Caroline. You're doing it!'

After the next contraction, she rocks back to squat in the water with her hand down between her legs. She breaks out of her dream-state with childlike surprise.

'I can feel something – and it's not me!'

'That's your baby, Caroline!' Lynne assures her, beaming. She's on the home stretch now. The next contraction redirects her attention, and her growl denotes she's getting ready to bear down with force.

I notice Vicki discreetly move a syringe, sealed in crinkly plastic, to a location by the mat. She anticipates a situation beyond my expertise. The hairs on the back of my neck stand up. The room is electric with anticipation: a new life is about to arrive. I prepare to record the event with Steven's digital camera.

But pushing isn't productive. Lynne guides Caroline to push for over an hour, checking the baby's heart rate at intervals. Then Lynne suggests she step out of the tub. Caroline isn't keen, but since the exhilaration has worn off, she relents. As she straddles the side of the bath, the hairy top of the baby's head is presenting in a rim of pink.

I fumble the camera. The room is so dark, I can't see if I'm framing things right. Another contraction comes. Caroline is now squatting by the bath and in one contraction There's the emerging head, the shoulders and then WHOOSH, a slippery baby is caught by the deft hands of a midwife.

Caroline sits on the mat with Steven to get a better view of their baby. Lynne declares the time of birth at 5.35am. Caroline's face is aglow, ecstatic that this moment has arrived. I take photos in the dark that do the moment no justice. The midwives unhurriedly assist Caroline to the bed to birth the placenta and examine the tear caused by such a fast exit.

There are no windows in the birth suite, but I know it's now dawn on Monday. I must get home in time for Paul to leave for work at 8 am. Best I drive now, while the adrenaline's peaking, than wait until my all-nighter catches up with me. I congratulate Caroline and Steven and promise to call later. I kiss

Lynne and Vicki goodbye and gather my things. As I head out the door Vicki grabs me, with both hands on my shoulders, eye to eye. 'Drive carefully, Jodie. Don't ruin a beautiful birth by falling asleep at the wheel.'

I take her advice to heart. Driving home, not pregnant, I think of my beautiful husband and children and how lucky I am to have them. Later, Kareena will deliver a casserole from her freezer, and mind the children for a few hours while I sleep.

One week later, a newspaper article titled, *A Labour of Love*, features a glowing Caroline and her newborn. She did it herself, despite enormous pressure to do it differently. There's a lot at stake at a birth, not just in terms of the black and white starkness of life and death, but also the in-between of emotional injury.

Much later, Caroline will tell me, kindly and gently, that my bellow, intended to save her voice, had intruded upon her mental state. And I'll thank her for telling me. I've accepted, without doubt, my calling is not to be a midwife or a doula.

We must understand that childbirth is fundamentally a spiritual, as well as a physical, achievement.
The birth of a child is the ultimate perfection of human love…

Dr. Grantly Dick-Read

29 KNOWING

Late January 2005

Once you know, you can't unknow. When you meet the people and hear their stories, you don't believe it can still be happening. And yet it is.

Mandalaine, Caroline's friend from Birthtalk, has taken great comfort from her birth story. Mandalaine has also had two caesareans and her third baby is due the same month. She can't afford to use Selangor Private Hospital and instead is attending Maternity Outpatients at the Royal.

At every prenatal appointment, care providers have directed her away from her preference for a vaginal birth and towards a scheduled caesarean. She would rather be at the Birth Centre, with her own midwife, access to tubs, and all the support of surgery and neonatal intensive care located right next door. But she isn't eligible. Frustrated, she posts online to a mainstream parenting forum about how no one at the Royal will accept she has a right to attempt a normal vaginal birth.

I sit at my desk, as usual. It used to be Paul's office, but it somehow became mine once I needed daily access to a phone and a computer. From this position I can write, check email, surf my online forums and see the yard through the windows with a 180-degree view. I can watch the children play outside or hear them playing elsewhere in the house. A platter of food on the end of my desk ensures they periodically return to my orbit. I can be very productive now that the children play together, aged almost five, three and nearly-two. The interruption is usually welcome and complements the different tasks I juggle at my desk.

The phone rings. It’s Kareena. She's in her car by the sound.

‘Am I interrupting? Got the kids with me. Can we drop in?’

‘Sure, I'm free. We’d love to play.’

‘See you in fifteen minutes!’

I hang up and face the state of my kitchen: crusty breakfast dishes in the sink next to last night’s pots and pans, and the mysterious slime on my kitchen doors. Then I see the piles of crumpled laundry on the couch that I rescued from last night's dew. Emergency clean up time!

I dump the laundry in my bedroom. No one will go in there. I scrape and rinse the dishes, flip the dish drawer closed and push START. I’ve wiped the bench and swept the floor by the time Kareena parks outside.

She sits on a kitchen stool to breastfeed her third baby, Lucas, born in her bathtub at home before Christmas. It was the natural step after Noah. Almost everyone I know, who’s lucky to have a choice, has a midwife at Selangor, the Birth Centre, or at home.

‘Your place looks nice,’ says Kareena. ‘How are so together?

‘Oh, I got the dishwasher on before you got here.’

Kareena enquires, ‘How’s Caroline?’

‘She’s doing great,’ I say. ‘I cooked for her yesterday. Shepherd’s pie, and a pot of chicken soup. Nothing fancy. Steven’s back at work now, and her mum will be there in a couple of days.’ Like me, she’s ready to test herself.

The older children are playing with water in the sand pit. They’re getting dirty but having fun and we don’t interfere.

Lucas has fallen asleep at Kareena’s breast. We admire the peaceful beauty of a sleeping baby, lips reflexively sucking after she pulls the nipple away.

'Can I put him down somewhere quiet?' she asks and I offer the futon in our bedroom. She stands effortlessly, baby cradled in one arm, and turns the knob on the door.

'What's all this?'

Then I remember the laundry, and I shrink. Caught in domestic deceit.

Kareena kicks the wash pile aside and makes a flat space.

'He's a good sleeper. We can sit here and fold.'

So, we tidy the clothes and talk about our families while the children play and the baby sleeps. It feels right. Women through the ages have done this. There's no word for the deep, calm connection I feel. A kind of caring that's all about doing.

'Jodie?' Kareena stops folding with a look of concern. 'Are you looking after yourself?'

'Why?' She has caught me by surprise. I almost say, 'Yes,' which would be a lie, and yet, 'No,' isn't truthful either. Truth is, I don't have a good routine of self-care.

'All the stuff you're juggling with your family. And Paul?'

My mouth falls open, but I have no reply. Kareena's frown breaks into a smile.

'Cos these are really sexy!' She holds my holiest grandma knickers up to the light and I see the extent of my deprivation. I snatch them away, laughing, 'Like you don't have ugly knickers at the back of your drawer? It was desperation underwear or nothing.'

'Then I choose nothing!' she retorts, and we buckle into hysterics. I let out a snort and the baby jumps, which makes us laugh harder.

We place the folded clothes into their respective drawers. I swell with love as we coax Kareena's family into the car to go home. I don't have a sister. Kareena's about the closest to having one as I've ever known.

'You smell good,' Paul leans in behind me at the computer. 'Am I interrupting?'

He lures me away to snuggle, but the children quickly find us.

'Muuummy, Daaaddy, I'm hungry!'

Our separate schedules make mornings and nights together difficult, so weekends during the day are our best time for intimacy. I prepare some cut fruit and cheese on a plate and put on a cartoon. It won't hold their attention for long. We have fifteen minutes at most. Lock the door, just in case.

I only learned to let go of my stuff since hitting my thirties. The advantages of living spontaneously, the way I choose to view this motherhood gig, are far reaching. Paul and I mash together like teenagers, achieving our objectives to the rat-tat-tat 'Muuummy!' on the bedroom door.

I step away laughing and my knees buckle. We giggle some more. Not so long ago I would have been too caught up in myself for this kind of frivolity.

'Mummy's busy right now!' Paul drawls as I quickly get dressed.

There's a rattle as Elijah, presumably, throws his whole body repeatedly at the door.

'I'm coming,' I call, amused by the irony. I let Paul bask in the afterglow while I attend to whatever it is Elijah finds so urgent.

I didn't always know it, but we'll make it, Paul and I. We'll grow old together.

My skin's different, and my muscle tone too. It's subtle but gives me cause to think we've conceived. Paul has a business trip scheduled next week. Eager to confirm before his departure, I do an early detection test. Negative. The next day I do another. Negative. I've wasted twenty dollars on two tests that confirm nothing, but I have a kind of knowing this time.

A week later, I greet Paul at the airport with the children. We kiss.

'Still think you're pregnant?'

On the way home we stop at an after-hours chemist for yet another over-priced test. I berate myself for wasting money on learning what I already know, until I see those magical blue lines. I present the stick to Paul, but the look on my face gives the punch line away.

Later that day, I get curious about the two spent tests at the bottom of the bin in the bathroom. I reach in, find the plastic paddles and flip them right side up. They'd failed to reveal what I knew to be true, but now both of them show faint blue lines. The weak hormone trace needed more time to activate the dye.

Patience. I sigh. The lesson is not lost on me.

I call and put my name on the Birth Centre ballot. It's just a routine designed to keep the numbers current. I already know I won't be using it this time.

'Congratulations,' says Elaine, 'I'm so sorry Tamara can't be your midwife.'

The baby who died at the Birth Centre, more than six months ago, was with Tamara. She's restricted to working the post-natal ward until the inquest is over. I'd sent her an email of support when I learned the news, but I haven't seen her since. She'd replied that she wasn't sure about catching babies anymore. My heart is heavy for her. My darling friend won't be my midwife this time.

Early February 2005

I recognise the name 'Mandalaine' on the *Natural Parenting* forum. Her scheduled caesarean is only a few days away, yet she posts seeking advice on vaginal birth after two caesareans. A forum member suggests:

> You still have time. Shop around for a new care provider. Are you in the catchment of any other hospitals? Even if you're not, call them anyway.

We all agree with Janet's advice:

> Don't turn up. Stay home and wait for labour as long as you can. Since you don't have a midwife or a doula, and you aren't prepared to stay home, then check yourself into the hospital as late as you dare, in established labour. They'll have no choice but to support your VBA2C.

No one suggests she should honour the arbitrary date for her 'elective' caesarean.

The day of Mandalaine's appointment arrives and she stays home. She suspects she's in early labour and leans on her network for reassurance. She updates us on the *Natural Parenting* forum, that she's having gentle, regular contractions. We post with lots of capital letters and exclamation marks.

> I'm so HAPPY for you! GOOD LUCK for your baby's birth! You can do it!!

Like so many times before, a spontaneous Blessingway begins as members post poetry and pictures and emojis and affirmations and light candles in a vigil until her baby is born.

She plans to give birth at Caboolture Hospital now. She enquired, and they're happy to admit her once labour's established. Apparently, Maternity at the Royal didn't receive that memo.

A few hours later, Mandalaine posts that two officers from The Department of Child Safety just knocked at her door, asking about her no-show for the appointment. They couldn't reveal whose complaint they were investigating, but it had to be her care providers at the Royal.

The forum explodes into heated debate. Dozens of new subscribers and anonymous voyeurs join the throng in the days that follow. *The World Today*, on ABC Radio, leverages Mandalaine's story to discuss what happens if you're pregnant and ignore clinical advice to have a caesarean. Apparently, in Queensland you're breaking the law. I get it, but it's a slippery slope.

A week later, Channel Nine's *A Current Affair* interviews Mandalaine about her joyful vaginal birth at Caboolture Hospital. By all reports, mother and daughter are doing wonderfully well.

30 STAKEHOLDERS

February 2005

The stakeholders' forum for the Independent Review of Maternity Services is held at Brisbane Girls Grammar. We meet at 9.30 am for tea and biscuits. I've just announced my pregnancy and there are congratulations from people who've heard the news. Many new faces are in the crowd, and excitingly, diversity, with Indigenous participants from outback Queensland and Thursday Island in the Torres Strait.

Midwives are usually identified by their motherly aura, big earrings or flowing skirts. They're generally discernible from consumers who carry an enormous handbag and a baby on their person. There are a number of doctors, predominantly male – their deportment identifies them, and expensive shoes. I deduce the remainder are health executives from all over Queensland addressing the conundrum of providing maternity care in their locality.

Consumers with babies take seats near the aisles and exits for easy escape. But we don't want babies to be invisible. They're the reason we're here! Besides, it takes weeks for nursing mothers to stockpile the milk they need to leave their infant with a carer. We also can't absorb the cost of childcare every time we attend an event. Unlike others in the room, we don't get paid for this.

Presenting to the forum are several successful maternity models from rural and remote communities, young parent's programs, Indigenous programs, urban team models. Expert midwives present on behalf of the Mackay and Brisbane Birth Centres and the Mater Mothers' midwifery group practice. Later, a panel of experts will be available for us to ask questions and give feedback. The Queensland President of the Australian Medical Association, Fertility Specialist and Obstetrician, Dr David Molloy, is on the list.

Jenny Gamble, behind me in the audience, leans in and whispers, 'I think I saw Dr Molloy doing an interview outside. Do you reckon he arranged his own media?'

Possibly, I do. He's on the TV a lot. It could be for something else.

After lunch, we settle in. Dr Molloy is the last to enter the auditorium. He strides down the aisle to the stage and his seat among colleagues on the expert panel. He introduces himself with a light-hearted joke that he 'just came from the golf course'. We glance at each other and fasten our seatbelts. This might be a bumpy ride.

Dr Molloy's reputation for exploiting statistics precedes him, and his representation on behalf of the AMAQ could be considered aggressive. More than once, he expressed criticism of 'natural birthers', implying they're risking their babies. It's common knowledge among staff at the Royal that he and some colleagues perpetuate an offensive joke, referring to the Birth Centre as 'The Killing Fields'.

I was once privileged to sit beside the inspirational Dr David Miller. He was a pioneering obstetrician in Byron Bay Shire for more than twenty years and the only rural doctor in Australia who happily attended homebirths. We were both presenting at a dinner with a regional waterbirth interest group. Through the course of the evening I'd asked for advice about agitating for change in hospitals.

He'd said, 'Treat it like chess. Observe the relative positions of all the pieces on the board and their defensive or offensive roles. You have to think three steps ahead and lead your opponent to the outcome you desire. Be patient, consider all options. Be prepared to change tactics if you lose your advantage.' Dr Molloy's style is more defensive.

Earlier, an Indigenous midwife explained how women in remote settings have diverse needs. There are some who live with domestic violence, substance abuse, malnutrition or alcohol dependence. They might avoid prenatal checks because hospitals don't cater to their language and culture. Hospitals can also be intimidating and judgemental places to go out of your way to visit. Vast distances make frequent travel a burden. Sometimes women turn up at their closest hospital in preterm labour, needing Medi-vac to a larger hospital. Many would prefer to give birth in their communities with their midwives, on their ancestral land.

'Yes, continuity of midwifery care does improve outcomes for women and babies,' says Dr Molloy. 'But it must embrace a multi-disciplinary approach.'

My mouth falls open. The audience starts to hum.

Behind me, Jenny says, 'I think he just agreed that primary care with a midwife is good for all women.'

Yes, I heard it, too.

'Women with complex needs require collaboration with multiple care providers: foetal medicine, obstetrics and neonatology, and midwives can facilitate that.' But he waxes paternalistic about overriding women's choices in order to rescue their babies. 'As the caesarean rate goes up perinatal mortality goes down.' Yes, but where does the balance lie? The murmur in the audience grows louder. Cesca's the first to yell out.

'What about informed consent? Mother and baby are a unit until birth! Caring for the mother *is* caring for the baby!'

I'm so glad Cesca had the guts to heckle.

My face grows hot and I blurt my anger, 'What about the rest of us?'

Dr Molloy adjusts his microphone and points at me.

'When five times as many mothers and twice as many babies die, compared to white Australia, there's an obvious need here!'

I'm humiliated. He implies I don't care about Indigenous mothers and babies. They have representatives in this room. Other women are calling out but Dr Molloy defends his pro-caesarean stance, 'If I can save one baby by performing two hundred and fifty caesareans, I'll do it. Especially when the child can sue for medical negligence up to 18 years later.'

Caroline stands, baby Samuel at her breast, 'Does that mean that my sons can sue for their unnecessary caesareans? Thank you, I'll pass that on to them.'

We may find his argument an offense, but he'll soon, unwittingly, give momentum to our cause.

Kath Solman has become a dear friend in the FBC committee and a rock of responsibility and action. She seems to understand the chaos of my workstyle and is able to slot herself into the cracks, sending reminders and posting updates so that nothing gets missed. I regularly joke, 'Kathy, we should go into business together.' She gives me a wry smile that probably means, 'That's a crazy-stupid idea, I'm not a fan of torture,' and humbly carries on.

Hannah announced her pregnancy by arriving at our September meeting with a yellow *Baby On Board* sign dangling around her neck. Kath's response of, 'Me too, Hannah!' added to the chorus of congratulations.

They both sailed through their first trimesters without too much nausea or fuss. The differences in their growing baby bumps is fascinating to us all. Hannah carries outward, her third baby, like most of us, showing almost immediately. It's Kath's third baby too, but she carries high, absorbing her baby, so that if you didn't know she was pregnant, you might have thought she was naturally shaped like a barrel.

By Christmas, both women have won in the ballot. They know they're fortunate, with only a quarter of applicants now able to access the Birth Centre.

In January, we're all expressing quiet concern. Kath's belly doesn't appear to have grown.

'My morphology scan's next week,' she shrugs.

'I'm sure all's well,' I reply, with no conscious reason to doubt it.

31 PROMISES

March 2005

While we wait for the report for the Maternity Services Review, Bruce insists we continue to meet with State and Federal members of Parliament and hospital health executives. This way, he says, when the findings are published, they'll be familiar with the context of the report.

We think we know what it'll reveal. That women who've experienced continuity of care with midwives are the overwhelmingly satisfied minority. Submissions from women who had obstetricians will be conspicuous by their absence, despite the general perception that obstetricians provide continuity of care. The report will note support for physiological birth in hospitals is restricted and women are being subjected to more interventions than can be justified in the name of safety. It'll note a sector of the population experience birth trauma. It'll note women are not blank slates coming into parenthood – we bring with us a history and a context that may include childhood and adult traumas like neglect or abuse, domestic violence, and sexual assault. But it'll be fantastic to have the issues presented officially, by an independent third party, for the consideration of policy makers.

Cautious optimism prevails in the birth reform community. The time's ripe for change. Since 1974, there have been nineteen Australian reviews of maternity services. Will this twentieth review drive change?

Members of Parliament are just regular people. They vary enormously in their personalities, knowledge and interests. But the majority of State and Federal MPs do care about reformist ideas and what happens to the people in systems they have the power to influence.

Peter Dutton, Liberal representative for Dickson since 2001, agrees to meet with us. He's probably aware proportionally more independent midwives and home-birthers live in Pine Rivers than any other electorate in South East Queensland, save the Noosa Hinterland, maybe.

His office is a museum of mementos from his time in the Police force. There's a couch with two opposing armchairs and a coffee table at their hub. We only recently bought our land in the Dickson electorate and don't actually live there yet, but as a future constituent I feel entitled to be here. I sit with the women on the couch, each with a belly or baby. Bruce takes one armchair, leaving the power seat for Mr Dutton. His assistant takes a nearby chair to document proceedings.

Our presentation is well orchestrated. Bruce says he's confident that Mr Dutton knows about Queensland's independent review of maternity services. We anticipate it'll express the desperate need to reform birth care in Queensland by upskilling and integrating midwifery models of care.

Bruce introduces us by name. We take turns to tell our stories as succinctly as possible – my spiel is second nature now. We have just one hour to make ourselves memorable so the Honourable Mr Dutton might lend his up-and-coming political weight to the status of midwives.

He knows his job is to listen, and he's very convincing. He shares that he's a father but doesn't give details.

'Look, I'm not an active advocate of homebirth,' he says, 'but I understand some women want it, and I can acknowledge that the insurance situation disempowers midwives. It's clear we need to provide more choices that address the unreasonable caesarean rate.'

Music to our ears.

Aside from the proactive support we received from The Greens, and from Ferny Grove Labor representative, Geoff Wilson, we also find an ally in Labor's Member for Lilley and future Australian Treasurer, Wayne Swan, a father with a close family of three adult children who all work in his Nundah office. Women in politics have been less receptive. However, the Governor of Queensland, Her Excellency, Ms Quentin Bryce, is a mother of five and the first Queensland woman to be admitted to the bar. She wrote Maternity Coalition a very thoughtful letter which Bruce followed up in his usual way, expanding his network of high-level support.

The report for the Queensland Maternity Services Review, called *Rebirthing*, declares everything we expected and more. One of their writers, Mary-Rose MacColl, takes up the gauntlet in editorials that highlight how maternity services in Australia are fraught with divisive practices. What women want, versus what women need, versus what's considered safe, versus what's proven safe, versus what feels safe. Whose wellbeing comes first – mother or baby, or hospital? The public discourse has begun.

We visit our land for a lazy weekend and some wholesome nature-play for the children. We keep enough basics to stay overnight, and maybe have a campfire. I always pack my camera as it's a lovely rural backdrop for family photos.

Under the shade of the tamarind tree, I take happy snaps of the children while they snack from a lunchbox of fruit. Paul has something on his mind.

'My boss wants to consolidate software engineering and I'm his first candidate,' he says. 'How would you feel about moving to Boston?'

I lower my camera. 'What, like forever?'

Paul looks bashful, 'They have excellent schools, I'm told.'

'And leave this?' I sweep my arm around our beloved farm. The basic brick cottage and rolling hills. We recently signed off plans for a house.

'That's the issue,' he nods, apologetic.

Curse his ambition! Paul and I have discussed his career options before, but never considered this scenario. On the other hand, the constant separation is hard, and the children are growing up. We could be together as a family for an extended while and what a luxury that would be.

My hand instinctively settles on the emerging curve of my belly. Already a stranger on the street has congratulated me. 'I'd be open to going for a while.'

Paul is surprised. 'You would? For how long?'

'How long do you need?'

'Two years?'

'The children're too young for school,' I say, 'but might be old enough to remember it. So long as we can come back?'

'You couldn't leave this?'

'I'm surprised you even ask.'

'How often does the perfect job present itself like this?'

'It would be perfect if it were here,' I pout.

'True,' Paul admits, 'but really, you would go, for a short time?'

I take a moment to think about it. Raising a young family is a time of immense change and the last four years have been action-packed. I've become accustomed to the churn. I'm not attached to our house, or our car. But here, this place, 'the farm' – I had an emotional reaction the day we drove past the For Sale sign. I knew immediately that this was a special place where we could make a beautiful life.

'It would be an adventure, right?'

'You'd be alright having the baby there?'

'I guess so.' I missed the Birth Centre ballot. Only this time, without Tamara; finally, I have a sincere reason to pursue a homebirth.

Reading my mind Paul asks, 'How do you find a midwife in Massachusetts?'

I say, 'Leave it with me. If I find one I like and trust, we'll go.'

32 REBIRTHING

April 2005

Tragedy arrives for one of our own in Friends of the Birth Centre. No sooner had I announced my pregnancy than Kath's ultrasound scan showed her baby has a terrible disorder and is growing minus a significant portion of his brain: a neural tube defect incompatible with life. The prognosis is that the baby will likely die in utero or survive only a few days after being born. Kath takes a week to think about it and decides to terminate.

Her midwife, Marg, organises a private room on the ward, away from the sound of crying babies, with professional trust to conduct the entire procedure herself. When Kath is a puddle of self-pity on the bed, Marg knows she can say, 'This baby deserves the same dignity and respect you gave your other children.' It kicks Kath off the bed and gets her moving to bring the labour on. She'll never forget her midwife, in both birth and death, as she swaddles sweet baby Christian, a tiny doll of 25 weeks gestation. Marg, who in all her career has never lost a baby, gives Kath all the time she needs to say goodbye.

Since 1995, Friends of the Birth Centre has always held a birthday party on June 12, or the nearest weekend. Usually it's a simple affair. A park with an appropriate play space is selected. Someone bakes a cake or buys one. There might be balloons or cheap books, gift-wrapped for the children, dressed in their FBC t-shirts. The midwives are presented with a bursary cheque for journals and professional development to whatever value FBC can afford. But for the tenth anniversary, something more significant is required.

Despite her loss, Kath is determined to continue coordinating events. She's the core of our team. Radio personality, Robin Bailey, continues to be our spokesperson. As a consumer group, we've learned and grown.

We want the BIRTHday Party, as we've begun to call it, to be a Celebration with a capital C. I'm leaving a lot of the planning to the team and getting on with the business of growing our last baby; culling to move abroad, keeping the family fed and clothed and supporting Paul's demanding career. My task for the BIRTHday Party is merely to be the historian, gathering materials for a tent museum reviewing the story of the Birth Centre.

It's low on my priority list.

Naively, I believe the report from the Independent Maternity Services Review will immediately kickstart reforms. Bruce is making headway on the Federal homebirth agenda, partnering with Maternity Coalition's National President, Justine Caines. He'll shortly fly to Canberra with Toowoomba midwife, Liz Wilkes, for the first of many briefings with the Senate. These are exciting times!

At the next FBC meeting, I take Melissa Fox aside to explain my intention to relocate to Boston for two years. She's taken aback.

'When will you go?'

'September.'

'You'll give birth in the States? How will that work?'

'I'll have a homebirth, at our own expense.'

'And what about FBC?' she asks, eyebrow raised.

'That's why I'm telling you,' I reply, 'in confidence, if you don't mind.' I take a moment to figure out what I'm going to say, 'Lis, you've been such an asset to FBC. The waterbirth rally was genius. I wondered if you'd be willing to be my proxy until the AGM, maybe even nominate to be president next year?' Melissa looks uncomfortable. She juggles her daughter onto the other hip and squares herself to face me. An honesty pose. I brace myself.

'Jodie, it's an honour to be asked, but I've decided to engage with Maternity Coalition and represent at the Mater. Maybe even help Bruce with the Federal agenda for reform.'

'Oh, I see,' I should have realised she's much too savvy for our little consumer group and of course the progressive agenda is closing the access gap and getting midwives autonomy of practice.

'Good for you, Lis. That's great.' I stutter. 'Who else would be willing to step in. Jo Smethurst?'

Melissa looks coy. 'Sorry Jodie, she's coming to Maternity Coalition with me.'

I understand. Those two are a powerful team, and Jo's prior experience in health advocacy has served the Queensland maternity agenda supremely this past year. I'll have to work harder to entice someone to take my baton.

When the *Rebirthing* report was released, a lot of media rolled off the back of it. Widespread reform and collaborative relationships between midwives and obstetricians shared the top of the list. Direct entry midwifery courses are to be reclaimed – since midwifery has been subsumed by nursing for almost 80 years. We feel validated by the media's attention and the reflection of public consciousness.

But the report is overshadowed by other news. A nurse in Bundaberg has blown the whistle on a suspected cover-up. A Queensland Health surgeon, dubbed "Doctor Death", Dr Jayant

Patel, is implicated in more than a dozen patient deaths. He has absconded to the United States, on a business class ticket reimbursed by Queensland Health. The Department is putting out fires, left and right. All the promised publicity for the *Rebirthing* report gets swallowed in a cyclone of health care hysteria. Premier Peter Beattie has been disgraced. Health Minister, Gordon Nuttal, will eventually resign following accusations of corruption. We've lost two years of work.

33 SCAPEGOAT

May 2005

Stepping off the travelators at the circular Toowong Shopping Centre always makes me giddy. I'm meeting Tamara at a cafe on the third floor. We haven't connected since before the tragic incident at the Birth Centre. She has, understandably, been rather reclusive.

She's punctual as usual and stands up as I approach so she can give me a long, warm hug. She looks tired. Her blond streaks are overdue for a retouch. The dark roots of her hair are shiny, with a dark fringe over her eyes. There's a set to her jaw I've never observed before.

'You look well,' she says. 'Are you feeling well? You look well.'

I see through her chit chat. How she talks more when she's nervous. How she didn't sleep last night. How she doubts herself now and worries that she always will. I want to wrap her up in cotton wool and take her pain away. We can't talk about what happened even though it was almost a year ago, because the inquest is still ongoing.

'And you look rested from your time off.'

'You're a liar, Jodie, but thank you.'

She gestures toward our table in the middle of the empty cafe and we each order something ordinary from the bread-heavy menu with two glasses of juice to wash it down.

'How long were you off work?'

'About six weeks while the investigation was going on. I'm relieving on the postnatal ward now, which I quite like. But things run over and over through my mind, you know. I'll never forget that day for the rest of my life.'

I reach my hand over and squeeze her arm, which feels superficial, but she looks up and smiles.

'Work has been great. They've provided grief counselling. I was doing my job to the best of my ability.'

'Of course. I can't even begin to imagine...'

Our food arrives, but neither of us are really here to eat. We have a mouthful each and I give Tamara every opportunity to talk.

'I've applied to go out west nursing. As long as I'm not attending births, I'm still employed by Queensland Health. I'm grateful. Actually, I'm excited. And for the sake of the Birth Centre, I need to move on. It's for the best.'

I read between the lines and nod.

'You always wanted to see more of Australia,' I say.

'I still do,' she plays along.

'We're leaving town too. For a little while.'

'Where are you going?'

'Boston.' I wait for her reaction. 'Well, near Boston.'

'For Paul?' she says, 'I'm not surprised. How long?'

'Two years. It makes sense we do it now, before the baby comes.'

'You'll be having a homebirth then?' Her mouth curls into a smile that reaches her eyes and I'm flushed with affection for her. Nice to see a little of the old Tamara back.

'Well, fortunately the first midwife I contacted has an excellent reputation and an open-door policy. I'll be 33 weeks when we arrive, but that's not a problem for her. We won't have much time to get to know each other, is all.'

'I'm sure everything will be fine.'

Tamara raises her glass as if to make a toast. Following her cue, I raise mine, and we clink.

'To travel,' she says.

'To travel,' I echo.

And in the back of my mind I hear her Unit Manager saying, *Sometimes babies die. And for all our technology, we still don't always know why.*

June 2005

I've promised to attend a play group in Roma Street Parklands with the *Natural Parenting* crew. The formidable JCF / Janet from the forum is in Brisbane. I'm keen to meet her and see if her online bluster matches her real-life persona. A number of other forum members are traveling to attend and I'm excited to meet them too.

Sometimes a rapport with an online friend doesn't translate once you meet in real life. Other times, an online bond doesn't exist, but an immediate connection evolves face to face. Maybe Janet will turn out to be a sweet, soft-spoken little pixie, and by meeting her in person her online personality will be less abrasive to me.

One cannot come empty handed to play group. And being a natural parent, I cannot bring store bought food. That would be social suicide. I have to make something from scratch that's worthy of the sharing table. I browse my stinky fruit bowl and empty fridge for inspiration.

I've two avocados and a lime – enough to make guacamole – and five minutes to get the kids out the door and be at the parklands on time. I chop and mash the slightly over-ripe avocados with one eye on the clock and the other on the children, but it gets done, and with just enough time to spare.

I park and corral the children toward the playground at the park, placing my home-made guacamole and corn chips down beside two similar offerings. Olivia introduces me to her guests, Janet and her husband. He's softly spoken, trailing after their three-year-old child.

Janet sits regally on a blanket with a circle of admiring women, her home-born baby in a wrap on her chest. I shake her hand and exchange a hug.

'So, you're Jodie Miller?' she says more as a statement than a question.

She has a large physical presence, medium length curly brown hair, and a clear, articulate voice. She wears a bold necklace and Doc Martin boots. When she laughs, she throws her head back with a unique, loud guffaw that you would recognise across a room. She's charismatic, her persona as large as her online presence. And, while I find nothing to *not* like about her, I confess, I'm intimidated.

Our conversations dance in circles, from our children, to recent discussion threads on the forum, to everything and nothing at once. I try to keep up, particularly with the political conversations between Janet and the other mothers, but the children pull me in all directions.

'Push me, Mummy,' on the swings, and 'Look at me, Mum!'

I eventually recognise their tired signs and take my cue to leave or risk a public meltdown. I return to collect my guacamole dish. All the food has been consumed with only crumbs and smears remaining. Except for mine. It sits there, grey and watery and completely untouched between two bowls that have been scraped clean. Shame washes over me as I remove my offending bowl. The acrid smell now evident after two hours in the sun.

Janet looks up. 'Guacamole, yum. My favourite!' She draws in the surrounding women with that unique laugh of hers. I should have tasted the dip. It would have been better to endure the embarrassment of arriving empty handed.

Through the twenty-minute drive home Janet's comment returns to me.

Guacamole, yum. My favourite!

Was she poking fun or was it a harmless quip? As the memory circles again and again my cheeks flush and my paranoia rises. Given the tension on the forum since Janet joined, I'm insecure enough to presume there was some sort of alpha-female sentiment behind it.

34 THE KILLING FIELDS

Late May 2005

The BIRTHday Party is two weeks away, and our Birth Centre is embroiled in controversy.

The AMAQ, on the Channel Nine news, has accused a midwife of endangering a baby. Dr David Molloy claims the midwife refused to allow specialists to intervene for a shoulder dystocia. He says the baby needed resuscitation, which could have long term consequences, including brain damage. It reeks of his agenda to undermine the Federal government's recommendation to upskill nurse practitioners, like midwives, to address labour shortages in the health sector.

Shoulder dystocia occurs when a baby's head is born but the shoulders become stuck on the mother's pelvic bone. If stuck for too long, compression of the umbilical cord can starve the baby of oxygenated blood. It occurs in about one in 150 births and is a leading cause of cerebral palsy. Every birth professional recognises this complication and must be prepared to intervene. There's no time to lose.

Several techniques can be performed. Failure to birth the baby after attempting several manoeuvres leads to a traumatic caesarean surgery where the baby's head must be pushed back through the cervix to facilitate abdominal delivery.

The midwife, we now know is Marg, recognised the signs and hit the emergency button. While waiting for the paediatricians, she didn't sit on her hands. She asked the father to assist in turning his wife over and proceeded to apply the woods screw manoeuvre.

The technique is to insert a hand into the vagina, and withdraw the baby's posterior arm then, with a finger on the other shoulder, rotate, or 'screw' the baby out. It isn't pleasant for mother, or baby. It risks breaking the baby's collar bone or dislocating a shoulder which can cause permanent nerve damage if it doesn't go smoothly.

Marg's intervention was successful, and the paediatricians arrived as the baby was born, limp but, fortunately, not cyanosed and blue. Marg didn't rush to clamp the cord, letting baby receive her oxygenated umbilical blood, and maintaining calm for the parents. Resuscitation and blood checks took place in an adjacent room. Baby was returned soon after looking pink and healthy. The father declared on the evening news they were satisfied with the outcome but, evidently, someone in the room lodged a vexatious complaint.

Days later, an article in *The Courier-Mail* states hospital executives have threatened to close the Birth Centre. Commissioner Tony Morris has been assigned to investigate Dr Jayant Patel in Bundaberg and other performance issues in regional hospitals, including a culture of concealment and bullying within Queensland Health itself. The Department is ultra risk-averse right now. My phone rings all evening fielding calls from women wanting to know if the Birth Centre will really shut down.

On Friday, hot off the furore caused by Jayant Patel, Dr Molloy addresses journalists from numerous media outlets, shamelessly describing how he and his colleagues call the Birth Centre, 'The Killing Fields'.

'That's a truthful nickname amongst the doctors, based on the number of near misses that leave people shaking their heads,' he says. 'I wouldn't have my own wife deliver at a Birth Centre.'

His comments are shocking and unfounded, but all major news channels broadcast the segment. My phone rings off the wall.

I talk first with Bruce, then Jenny Gamble, now Queensland President of the College of Midwives. She has already spoken with Gay Hawkesworth, the Secretary of the Nurses Union, and they would like an opportunity to address the media.

'FBC has a meeting tomorrow morning,' I say, 'with around twenty parents and their children. What if we made it a press conference?'

It's agreed. All the news channels are invited to Windsor House at ten o'clock the next morning. All the birth groups bring their rent-a-crowds and arrive by nine for a briefing. Of course, babies and children are welcome.

Saturday morning is a swarm of solidarity. Friends of the Birth Centre, Maternity Coalition, the Home Midwifery Association, the Australian College of Midwives and the Queensland Nurses Union share an inaugural cup of tea. Our numbers have swelled to about fifty mothers, plus a gaggle of children and babies. The media crews are punctual. Bruce, Gay and Jenny address the cameras.

'It's not an issue of safety,' says Jenny. 'This is a turf war. This is about private, specialist, obstetricians shoring up their income for the future.'

My one line to the camera is awkward, as usual, but our collective response leads the news that night. Commissioner Tony Morris states, 'I think what you've got here is Dr Molloy trying to drive a wedge between doctors and nurses.'

We couldn't have hoped for more.

Dr Molloy retracts his statement in Monday's issue of *The Courier-Mail* and promises he'll never use the slur again. I worry that this incident will impact our 10th BIRTHday event. Preparations are irreversibly underway. We've sold stalls, designed a t-shirt, and the newsletter is with the printer. We plead with our membership, asking them to write Letters to the Editor and approach their regional free press for a photo opportunity and a blurb about the Birth Centre's decade anniversary. Have we done enough to draw a crowd, or will the hype have harmed our public image? All the team's hard work could be for nothing.

June 2005

It has been almost 18 months since the promise of a Birth Centre for the Gold Coast. Bruce and I carpool to the inaugural planning day. The one-and-a-half hour drive gives us time to define our vision.

'This sets a precedent of sorts,' Bruce says, 'that the government's telling a hospital what to do. Usually they dole out the money, and hospital executives decide how to spend it. They might not be ready for this.'

We arrive at the Gold Coast Hospital, where we meet Deirdrie Cullen and members of the newly formed Friends of the Gold Coast Birth Centre. This is the first time hospital executives, nursing and midwifery staff, obstetrics, neonatology, consumers and other stakeholders have all gathered to create a vision of an ideal model of Birth Centre care and how it might intersect with other hospital services.

An executive thanks the room for their attendance saying, 'Ideally, the whole of maternity could be a Birth Centre.' The room breaks out in vehement disagreement. We know that's not how it works in a tertiary hospital with a responsibility to educate young doctors, nurses and midwives. A Birth Centre demands that the scale remain small and intimate, with more privacy, flexibility and trust in the midwifery staff than you find in the hospital workforce. That's the whole point. Woman-centred care, by definition, makes the woman the decision-maker and care providers cater to her. If this Birth Centre can be an all-risk model, where midwives, obstetricians and paediatricians work collaboratively, all women could benefit. Especially those from cultural minority groups, or women with complex reproductive histories.

We fill sheets of butcher's paper with positive words. We draw mind maps and flow charts and lists. We share our ideas freely, in a safe space, expertly facilitated by Dr Denis Walsh – actually a Doctor of Nursing. And at the end of the day I drive home to Brisbane inspired by our day. Riding with me is Jenny Gamble, animated as always. She brings me down from my high.

'All the talking today will come to nought,' she says. 'They're not going to adopt an all-risk model for a start. That would be too bolshy for a hospital that's never had a Birth Centre before. They'll replicate what exists in other hospitals, and innovation will be left to the individuals swimming upstream in that system. Today was about mediocrity.'

'Surely not!'

'Oh, they'll start with all sorts of idealism. But as we've seen before, obstetric oversight will gradually ratchet up the intervention and strangle innovation.

'When we see midwives regulated as a profession in our own right, not managed as employees under nursing, there's potential to make a maternity system that's woman-centred. We're hobbled by Medicare being a Federal concern in Australia, and hospitals run by the State. Birth Centres are nice in theory, but the evolution of maternity care, midwifery especially, doesn't lie in them.'

I puff my chest. 'What about Deirdrie then, who formed an FBC for the Gold Coast, being a VBAC mum and all? She's advocating for a Birth Centre she'll never get to use.'

'Isn't that the story for all of us? We're not doing this for ourselves. We do this for our friends and our daughters. We do this to make something right that's wrong.'

35 BIRTHDAY

June 2005

Our relationship with the Royal has never felt so tenuous. The midwives deliberate over every clinical decision. A report on the Birth Centre is harsh, identifying a toxic 'culture of blame, unsupportive of open disclosure of errors and adverse events.' Every aspect of the model is under scrutiny and its future isn't assured.

Now we must forward our FBC newsletter to the hospital for approval. My President's Report is reviewed, and occasionally questioned. Where did I obtain my facts? We're throwing all our resources at promoting the festival in Roma Street Parklands, our biggest event yet, but don't feel confident of success.

Nothing about the Birth Centre's milestone has been issued by the Royal's public relations team. They leave the media release to us. Our supporters write letters, make calls, and send emails of solidarity which is exactly the publicity boost we need. On the day, our festival attracts over three thousand people, the largest show of support for midwifery Australia has seen to date.

There are queues for the merry-go-round, jumbo slide and king-sized jumping castle. There's face painting and all sorts of fun and games on the lawn. The rows of market stalls with tidy white marquees were worth the cost to make the event look good. And the midwives are deserving of their day of adulation. Melissa Fox delivers a sack containing the letters of support to Marg and Karen – padded with newspaper for effect – in front of an adoring crowd. And on behalf of the committee, she presents a tiny gold dragonfly on a delicate chain for Kath – her symbol of baby Christian.

For the third year in a row we confront the media. Bruce, Jenny and I offer a good half dozen sound bites. We congratulate ourselves on our accumulated skills.

With the festivities over, I leave the parklands inflated by the day's success. As the stall holders lug their wares away and the gang arrives to pull down the marquees, I see Kath and Dani cleaning the public toilets.

I stop at the door, 'The park janitors'll do that.'

'We save $300 if we do the bins and toilets ourselves.'

'What can I do to help?'

Kath motions at my belly with her gloved hands, 'There's nothing you need to do.'

'Thank you,' my voice cracks. The women of FBC powered the whole event. My contribution was pathetic, and they don't begrudge me a thing.

July 2005

Mum calls out of the blue. She's visiting her two closest sisters, Betty and Wanda, in Deception Bay. I'm welcome to visit and please bring the children.

I drop everything and go. It's my chance to tell Mum in person about our hiatus to America. I worry about how she'll receive this news. That we're in the audience of my aunts isn't ideal, but it's better than over the phone.

The three women greet us effusively and touch my tummy. Mum seems at ease with her sisters. I yearn for her to have that ease with me, and it'll taunt me later, on the drive home while the children sleep.

'My babies! How are we all? Nana has missed you!' She bends down, pulling Elijah and Ruby into a squeeze. They giggle, then run off to play with the toys Aunt Betty keeps for her grandchildren. Kyle wants to breastfeed, so I let him.

Mum looks away, 'Are you *still* doing that?'

I shrug. 'It works for us.'

'How old is he?' asks Wanda.

'Just turned two. We've night weaned. Finally, we got one that sleeps.' I try to make it sound light, but I can sense disapproval from my aunts that the child is still sleeping in our bed.

Betty offers jam roly-poly to the children, which will spoil their lunch, but I say nothing. She asks the usual, 'How's Paul? Still doing all that travel?'

'Yes, but we have a solution to keep us together.'

'He's changing jobs?' she asks.

'Not exactly.' I glance at Mum, unsure if this is the right moment. 'It's an opportunity inside his company. We're going to the US for two years.' The three sisters exchange a look. There's silence while they digest this information.

'Where?' asks Betty.

'Massachusetts. Near Boston.'

Mum hasn't said a word. We sit sipping tea and nibbling cake, waiting for someone to speak.

Finally, Mum declares, 'But...it's so far away!'

I hear her to my core. Underneath her lament lies a gap of two years in our history. A baby was born, and toddlers became children who grew bigger in her absence. Two years of me missing her too. And now I'm imposing another two years in which another baby will be born, and small children will grow, and we won't get that time back. It hurts, but I can't plan my life around hers.

'The time'll fly, Mum. We'll keep in touch. You're welcome to come visit. All of you!' I gesture to Wanda and Betty. But I know Mum will never step on a plane to visit us. Not a long-haul flight over the Pacific Ocean, and a connecting flight to the east coast. She's always been afraid of all that. And since she left

Dad, I feel an absence, not just of her, but of my comprehension of her. Maybe, by the time we return, Mum and I'll be ready to talk about it, like adults. We've no choice now but to wait for that.

36 HAPPY LANDING

September 2005

I take the exit to Needham, in the New England region, and turn onto the 'wrong' side of the road. It's my first time driving in the US. Accustomed to left-hand drive, I have to override my reflexes.

'This feels so scary!'

Paul is more practiced than me. 'You're doing fine.'

My heart is racing. New car, new country, new rules, and our precious family on board. But the road is empty this morning. Paul pulls out a map and scans for a street sign. Tidy two storey wooden houses with black shutters and dormer windows line the streets. All have cute steps to even cuter front porches.

New England today is all green lawns dotted with brown and gold leaves under magnificent flaming oak trees, so different to our sub-tropical home. It was warm when we arrived in mid-September, but a week later, the nights were cool enough to trigger the autumn change. I glance at my brood in the rear-view mirror. I can't wait until they see snow!

'What the? Kids, look!' I point out an enormous black spider on a cotton-wool web decorating the front of a house.

Paul chuckles at my naivety. 'Soon there'll be jack o'lanterns, and black cats everywhere. Have you forgotten the baby's due date is Halloween?'

The children are restless. We pull over and check the map again.

'Why are we stopping, Mum?'

'Are we there yet?'

'I need to pee.'

'Can you hold on a bit longer? We're nearly there.'

We continue past a park, a school, another boulevard of leafless trees, and then I see it. On the corner, in the front yard of a typical New England house, a sandwich board sign, festooned with blue balloons, says:

It's a boy!
9lbs 6oz
BORN AT HOME
2.15 am Tuesday Sept 12
mother and baby doing well
BirthDay Midwifery
555 555 555

'This has got to be it.'

We park in the shade of an enormous cypress tree. My belly is the size of a basketball. I have to open the car door wide and step both legs out together to avoid triggering sciatica pains. This is my fourth pregnancy in six years and the discomfort is weirdly normal.

Nancy and I have spoken on the phone only twice. Someone on Babycenter.com recommended her when I'd posted asking for a midwife in the north Boston area. I'd liked her on the phone. Now it's time to meet in person.

We walk up three steps to a shiny black door. The glass is plastered with baby photos, and couple photos, and lots and lots of bellies. A warmth washes over me remembering the hallway of the Birth Centre. I ring the doorbell and Nancy appears, more petite than I expected, but humming with an energy that must not be underestimated. I can't place her age and don't try. Some people are ageless.

'J-ou-die, hello!' she chirps, shaking our hands, 'and you must be Paul. And this is your bea-u-tiful family? Welcome!'

She shows the children the singing and dancing animatronic pumpkin decorating her entry, like nothing they've ever seen before. Then, business-like, she guides us all downstairs to a converted basement and a classroom space with a wall of books where she conducts pre-natal classes. She brings some toys for the children and helps us settle them on the floor. Then, leaving the door open, she leads Paul and me into the adjacent room.

Nancy apologises for having the heater on. 'I wanted this space to be warm when you got here.'

I think it's lovely. I take the cosy seat by the radiator. My belly hangs so low now that I must part my knees and cross my ankles to be comfortable. Paul takes the cane daybed against the wall. Nancy sprinkles dried apricots and walnuts into a dish and places it in front of me.

'Go ahead and snack, we have quite a lot to get through.' She chatters calmly as she takes my blood pressure, then glances over my file from Australia. I learn she has children, young adults in college, and she was a speech therapist before her first child's caesarean birth changed the course of her career. Her hands are warm and her eyes full of humour. I glance at Paul and can tell he likes her too.

She ignores the ultrasound transparencies but reads the summary statement which declares the baby is the right size, placenta is ideally located and there's adequate amniotic fluid. She says to us both, 'Everything exactly as it should be.'

Nancy takes out a form, asking for details about my previous births. Have I ever been a smoker, a drug user, a risk taker? How many times have I been pregnant, and have I ever miscarried? Were my other babies all born on time, how long was each labour, were there any complications, all breastfed easily? How many menstrual periods have I had between babies, how long did they last and how heavy the flow? Are my pap tests up to date? Describe a typical day from waking to sleeping and the food and drink I consume. How much exercise do I get? How many times a day does the baby move? She turns her attention to Paul.

'You two seem like a great team, and I can see you're involved with the children. Paul, I'd love to hear your side of the story. What were your babies' births like?'

Paul is taken aback. He's attended many prenatal checks with me and rarely been asked what he thought.

He explains how our babies were born in a Birth Centre, waterbirths, the same midwife for all three. He appreciated being able to stay overnight in the double bed to help with the stress of early breastfeeding. He's too humble. In labour, he'd walked with me, applied heat packs, rubbed my back, and supported my weight during contractions. His was the only voice I wanted to hear say, 'You're doing great,' or, 'You're amazing!'

'I couldn't have done it without him,' I say, as if to defend him.

'I'm so glad to hear it,' Nancy chirps. 'Because some dads can be a bit squeamish.'

She directs more questions to Paul. Did we use birth control, are we still having sex now, when was the last time? He looks bashful, but answers, unaccustomed to the invasion of privacy that women accept as normal.

Some of her questions are unexpected – and after three pregnancies I thought I'd heard them all – but we're happy to give all the information she wants. With only a few weeks to go, my every hope is pinned on Nancy being my midwife. I know enough about birth in American hospitals to be certain I don't want to use one, except by absolute necessity.

'Well Jou-die,' she says as she closes my file, 'I'm not in the business of denying my services to any candidate who wants a homebirth. I liked you from the moment you called. I admire that you've been working to progress midwifery in Australia and since you're in excellent health with a perfect history I would be delighted to be your midwife!'

Paul and I sigh with relief.

'There's just one important thing I have to tell you.'

I suck in my breath. 'O-kay.'

'Since your babies all came on time it isn't likely to be an issue, but the middle weekend of November is my fiftieth birthday. That's exactly two weeks after your due date so if your baby hasn't come by then I'm afraid to say, I won't be available myself. You'll get to meet my back-up midwife, in due course.

I exhale and say, 'Nancy, I seriously doubt there'll still be a baby in here by then.'

She looks pleased. 'I like your attitude.'

37 BIOPHYSICAL PROFILE

October 2005

The house phone rings. It's not a sound we often hear. Our circle is small and our Aussie friends are surely asleep at this hour.

I make a tentative, 'Hello?'

'It's me. I'm coming home. We need to talk.'

Twenty minutes later, Paul arrives with a Boston Market dinner in hand, and an irritable look on his face. He cracks the top off a beer from the fridge and turns to face me, concerned.

'What's it?'

'Looks like I'm heading back to Brisbane this weekend.'

He takes a swig from the bottle.

'For how long?'

'A bit over a week.'

I blink. 'Is that all?'

'What do you mean, is that all? Could the timing be any worse?'

'Better now than later.'

'But with you getting so close?'

'I'm 37 weeks. I'm not anywhere near close.' I touch the underside of my tummy and recall the sensations in the days before labour. The discomfort right there above the pubic bone, so sensitive that the rub of my loosest waistband drove me crazy. Right now, my tummy is high and tight. Sitting is relatively comfortable. This baby isn't coming anytime soon. Paul doesn't look so sure.

'Besides, the midwives come to me, remember? I just have to pick up the phone.'

'Do you want Shelly to come sooner?'

Shelly's his niece who works in childcare. We bought her a ticket to come a week after our due date. She's great with the children and fantastic emotional support for me. If the baby hasn't arrived by then, all the better. We'll need a support person for the children while Paul and I are busy with the birth.

'No. We'll visit the library and go to Nancy's mothers' group. We'll be fine.' Truth is, driving still scares me, but being trapped at home scares me more.

'If anything changes, I'll be on the first plane home.'

'Honestly, it feels far away, Paul. You go. We'll be fine.'

Two days later, he's gone. I work hard to keep busy, and not think about what could go wrong.

At my next my prenatal visit with Nancy, I walk the children up to her porch. The musty smell of fallen leaves rises from the damp. There's a bright orange wreath hanging on the door, and a new picture in the glass. A young couple, clearly expecting, have painted her belly to look like a pumpkin.

Nancy approaches before we knock and swings the door wide to a blast of warmth, and the smell of fresh baked bread. She hugs me warmly, and greets the children in turn, expertly recalling their names. Her home is a blaze of orange.

'Welcome back!' she trills. 'Do you need the washroom after your long drive?'

She shows us down the hall to the 'washroom' and I see a spacious bathroom, a toilet and hand basin, plus a large shower behind a curtain. It's a generous visitor's bathroom. I explain the meaning of 'washroom' to an Australian, usually just a toilet off a laundry, and Nancy laughs.

'A couple of women've had babies in here.'

I'm incredulous that women wouldn't prefer their own home, having hired a midwife and all.

'Sometimes they don't,' she says. 'Maybe they're renovating, or live with the in-laws, or their apartment is small, and they worry about disturbing neighbours.'

'Two babies were born here, and three in the bedroom. One was a couple I'd never met before. They turned up at my door in active labour because their obstetrician wouldn't negotiate with them.'

'That's not fair on you!'

'What am I gonna do? Turn them away? The mother and baby deserved a good birth. And it was. So much stress for no reason.'

She presents me with the midwife's calling card – a urine dipstick.

'Let's start by checking your protein. You know what to do with this.'

She calls the children, 'Who's going to the bathroom with Mom?'

A child's potty sits opposite the adult pedestal with a fluffy mat between. Beside is a rack of children's books. I flick through them, noting a worn copy of *Walter the Farting Dog* and an English translation of the quirky Japanese book *Everyone Poops*. I show the children, eliciting peals of laughter.

I emerge and present the dipstick, which is changing colour before my eyes.

'Sugar is a little high,' Nancy compares it to the chart on the jar. 'Binged on Halloween sweeties?'

'I had some barley sugar in the car – I skipped lunch.'

She cocks a knowing eyebrow, and clucks, 'Yes, it's a hazard alright. You've got to look after yourself. Keep some almonds in the car. Your protein was perfect last week so I'll give you the benefit of the doubt. Bring the children downstairs and let's get started.'

After taking my blood pressure, Nancy suggests I lie down on the daybed against the wall while she measures my belly from pubic bone to fundus, exactly as Tamara did.

'Thirty-seven centimetres for thirty-seven weeks – perfect! Did you know this is one of the few times we use metric?'

Nancy prods my belly deeply with her confident fingers and announces that the baby is optimally positioned and undescended.

'I bet that's a relief – with Paul away.'

'I'm not worried. I don't feel close yet.'

Nancy pulls out a weird contraption I've never seen before. She attaches the whole apparatus to her head via a metal bracket that presses against her temples and behind her ears. On her forehead is a protuberance like a tiny trumpet. She inserts earpieces like a stethoscope, and then looks at me, taking in the surprise on my face.

'Do I look like I'm from outer space?' she laughs. 'It's called a fetoscope and if I place it correctly on your tummy, I can hear your baby's heartbeat through the bones of my skull, no need for a Doppler.'

'You don't use a Doppler?'

'Oh, they have their place. I use one during labour, but I'd rather avoid invading the baby's space. I recently read a paper describing how unborn babies move away from the sound pulses sent through the amniotic fluid, so maybe it's uncomfortable for them.'

Nancy leans in with the horn on her head and presses it deeply into the tissue of my belly. She withdraws and then presses in again, at an incrementally different location, a look of deep concentration on her face. Suddenly her eyes light up and she raises a finger like a conductor and beats it quickly with the rhythm of my baby's heart. I can't hear it myself, but the smile on her face gives me comfort that all's as it should be. She obviously loves what she does.

She pulls my shirt down over my belly and offers her hand so I can pull myself up to sitting.

'This being your fourth time around, are you prepared to catch your baby?'

'Excuse me?'

'With Paul away, I just wondered if you know what to do. Not saying it'll happen, but have you ever thought about what you'd do if the baby started coming too fast?'

I've been in the business of collecting birth stories for long enough to have heard plenty of 'oopsie' stories. Women who'd caught their babies in the toilet, not realising they were in labour, women whose babies were born in the car, or by the side of the road, or in the ambulance on the way to the hospital. I remember Rianna, but I don't believe it'll happen to me.

'Well, promise to at least prepare a Go-Bag, just in case. Teach the children how to dial 911. If it does happen, turn up the central heating and make a nest on the floor with some blankets, okay? I don't know what winter is like in Australia, but here it's essential to keep the baby warm.'

After three protracted births, I seriously doubt a precipitous labour will happen to me, but agree I'll pack a bag to ease her mind.

'The next consultation will be in your home. My colleague, Heather Laier, will attend you. She's the one I call if I ever can't make it to a birth.'

On the way out, Nancy grabs her new digital camera, the size of a credit card.

'Would you like me to take your photo? I bet it's the last thing you'd think to do, yourself now and the children.'

She's right. We've been here several weeks now. But with Paul away for a few more days, I'm still in a whirl. We stand in Nancy's garden, the children close to me. At the last second, I pull up my shirt and bare the skin of my enormous tummy to the cool autumn air.

We both laugh and Nancy takes my picture.

It snows on Ruby's birthday. Just a flurry which melts quickly, but it's enough to make the day special, considering we have no friends here to help us celebrate.

Halloween arrives. Our neighbours show Paul and the children how to Trick or Treat. I stay home to greet guests with a bowl of ethical, non-candy treats – character band aids, bead bracelets and novelty toothbrushes. With growing shame, I observe their falling faces as I present my bowl of 'treats' to the costumed children at my door. Their adult chaperones express surprise that my enormous belly isn't a costume.

'Oh, it's real?' they fumble. 'When's your baby due?'

'Today.' My accent sounds foreign to my own ear.

'Ooh, well,' they scramble, 'good luck with that. We'll be off!'

The cultural gap is a chasm. I've disappointed my visitors, missing an opportunity for a visual gag. What a shame I'll never have this chance again.

November 2005

Halloween disappears with the dawn, and I haven't produced a baby. A week later, Paul's niece, Shelly, arrives on a flight from Brisbane. I've never been more than a few days overdue and my discomfort grows day by day. To remedy my cabin fever, Paul drives us all to Cape Cod. It's two hours from home and a small risk, but the children take off their shoes and walk on the icy grey shore, and we enjoy the sensory nostalgia of the ocean after being indoors for weeks on end.

At 40 weeks and 9 days, Nancy offers to take me to the hospital for a biophysical profile – to check the baby's wellbeing – but I decline. Baby is active as ever and I'd rather not test fate.

Two days later, Nancy calls one last time to check on me before leaving on her birthday holiday. I tell her that my bowels are active and I'm having mild, irregular contractions.

'I could hold off a few more hours,' she offers, but I object. You only turn fifty once and her friends and family have travelled for the occasion. All I can think is, what if she waits and I don't go into labour? The pressure would be too much. I insist she have a good time. When I put the phone down, my contractions step up a notch and I try to calm my demons.

Anticipating a long night, Paul and I go to bed early. But with contractions coming every 10 minutes, I know sleep will be elusive. I decide to call Nancy's colleague, Heather, and warn her something might happen in the middle of the night.

It's 11 pm and I've woken her. She gruffly tells me she'll have to drop her son off on the way. I don't feel reassured. Paul lights the fire in the living room and sleeps on the couch while I pace and potter and try to conjure the strength of all my women friends on the *Natural Parenting* forum.

Hungry, I bite into a banana, and promptly throw it up. I'm on the cusp of active labour but keep fixating on Heather moving her sleeping child in the middle of a subzero night. I'm waiting until a decent hour to make the call.

I can feel the contractions right through to my bottom and I don't like it one bit. There's an interim sensation, that I realise is my cervix opening, which I've never felt before; so, I know these contractions are doing good work. Unable to sit and rest, I conserve my energy by kneeling on a pillow on the floor, bent forward over the cushion on the couch. It's not dignified, but who's watching? I bury my face in the cushion to muffle my groans and not wake the rest of the household.

Giving in to tiredness, I drift in and out of sleep in a nest of pillows on our couch, then wake at 6 am feeling nothing. Labour has stalled.

'The most important meal of the day,' says Paul, placing a cooked breakfast before me with eggs and beans and bacon. I push it away. Paul eats it with gusto.

'I'm going upstairs, if that's okay,' I say to Shelly and the children. 'The baby will probably come today.'

The children cheer, and I'm grateful this is a normal day for them. Paul and I leave them in Shelly's capable care and retreat to the bedroom to wait for labour to pick up where it left off.

I want to lie down on the bed and rest, but I have to stand during contractions, or the pain is unbearable. Paul reminds me to pee, so now and then I oblige.

Around lunchtime, during yet another toilet visit, I have to vomit. Simultaneously, my membranes release and I have to discard my clothes. Deja vu. The fluid is nice and clear.

'Let's call Heather,' I say and, forty minutes later, two cars are parked in our drive: Heather and her student midwife, Maggie. After preliminary hugs and welcomes, they discreetly bring all their equipment in and quickly get set up. Inside our closet they plug in a heated infant resuscitation tray and ambu bag, because Paramedics don't always carry equipment for newborns. I'm reassured they're prepared for a compromised baby, but confident we won't need it. Maggie lays out some disposable absorbent mats on the carpet by the bed and bathroom. I always wondered how they contain the mess.

The midwives are ready for something to happen, but labour progresses slowly, like each time before. I'm finally finding my zone. Now that Heather's here in our space, she seems warm and earthy and I like her. Paul is doing a great job at birth support, so Heather sits in the rocking chair in the corner and Maggie sits on the floor beside her, chatting casually between contractions.

'I'm sorry Nancy couldn't be here,' says Heather, 'but I had a feeling, when we first met, that I'd be your midwife.'

I'm not usually one for woo-woo, but being so far from home and everything familiar, I find her premonition reassuring. I continue to pace and lean into contractions and make conversation in the gaps. Heather and I share an interest in gardening. She has several fruit trees in her yard. I tell her about the orchard on our 'farm', and how we're building a house there. When Elijah was born, Tamara had saved his placenta, which I'd planted in a pot under a lime tree. Later, I added a mandarin tree for Ruby's placenta. We'd kept Kyle's in the freezer and planted it with an orange tree when we bought the land, then I'd planted the other trees with it. I'm sad that the tradition won't continue this time, but I'm content to add another tree to the collection (minus placenta) when we return home.

'Do you think we could plant a tree in your garden?' I ask Heather, 'with this baby's placenta? Is that weird?'

'I would be honoured,' she coos. 'Actually, I've reserved a space for a special tree. I've always wanted a weeping cherry.'

My heart flutters. Paul and I know it well from our time in Japan.

'I'd like that very much,' I say. A tree like that would not thrive in our Brisbane climate, but it's the perfect tree for our little American.

I can't help it; I cry like a baby.

'Oh look, she's weeping,' says Heather without judgement. And as I sob, a huge weight lifts, and the tension in the hammock of my pelvis seeps away. 'Oh honey,' she coos, 'let it all out.'

Immediately, my labour changes gears and warmth trickles down my leg to the absorbent mat underfoot. We won't be waiting much longer to meet our baby. I hear the children downstairs watching *The Wizard of Oz* and I slide into a familiar, liminal, dream space. I see Glinda, the Good Witch of the South. She says the Munchkins are coming to see me. Click your heels, Dorothy. There's no place like home.

Time passes, and Heather rocks gently in the chair. She asks if I'd like her to sing. And in a tuneful, clear voice she performs a birthy folk song, which makes me weep harder and open up some more. Soon, I'm kneeling on the floor with the support of a chair. I hear my moaning change tune and my conscious mind knows what comes next. I catch myself tensing and resisting, thinking NO!

Heather says, 'Push if you want to.'

I grunt, 'I don't want to.'

'Then it's all right not to push. Let your body do the work.'

After a couple more contractions, I can no longer hold back and I have to commit to pushing. I feel the baby's head move through my pelvis. I take it slow, pushing only as much as I have to, no more. The Doppler reports a reassuring heart tone, I figure I can take my time. But then, with the head about to crown, Heather offers to bring in the children.

I puff and blow, stretched to the max, but could happily stay like this rather than push through the intensity of crowning. The children enter the room in a bustle of noise, climbing up on the bed and settling in for the show. I can't see them, they're behind me, but I can sense how excited they are.

'If you prop one knee up, you can receive the baby yourself,' says Heather.

I appreciate her suggestion, but I need both hands to grip the chair.

'Paul can do it.' He's already close enough to have the honour. I gather my reserves for what I hope will be just a few more agonising pushes, and then we'll meet our baby.

It's a long time between contractions, and I wait with dread. Finally, I remind myself to embrace the experience. This is our last baby. And as the next surge builds, with a white-knuckle grip on the chair, I howl 'YEEEESSS!' and push through the burn until her head is born.

Behind me, two-year-old Kyle declares, 'Mummy, poo, baby!'

The mood lifts and we laugh. Our non-talker made his first joke!

Heather moves in for perineal support. Baby has her fist under her chin and an elbow protruding in front of her chest. Ah, the mysterious bottom-pain! One final push and her body slithers out into Paul's waiting hands, along with all the fluid and gunk dammed within my body and hers. She cries, and Paul passes her back through my legs, tar-like meconium smears his hands, and vernix coats her body. Born at the perfect time.

Heather wraps the baby in a warm towel and suddenly it all feels real. Oh, how much I needed to hold her! She's healthy and pink. We check that she is indeed a girl and name her Dawn. She's utterly, utterly perfect.

The umbilical cord is long and spiralled, like an old-fashioned telephone cord. We honour it by taking a photo. Dawn nurses effortlessly while we wait for the placenta to come. We invite big brother, Elijah, to cut the cord.

I was disappointed that Nancy couldn't be here, but developed the same immediate rapport with Heather, and all went exceedingly well. As Heather tucks me into bed, she leans in and kisses me on the cheek saying Tamara's exact words.

'Thank you for the honour of being your midwife.'

38 BLACK ICE

January 2006

We've experienced our first white Christmas and built our first snow man with the children. We're delighting in the pure-wonder whiteness of our own backyard, with picture-perfect trees balancing snowy nests on branches and a slope at exactly the right pitch for play on a saucer sled.

Nancy and Heather both host monthly mothers' groups, occurring fortnightly in relation to each other. They're compulsory events for my extrovert heart, accustomed to the frequent company of other mothers. Today it's at Heather's, but it's snowing. Why should I let that stop me?

Driving in snow is an uncommon experience for most Australians. I feel certain I've taken the correct exit off the freeway to Reading, but I'm confused by the white sheets of the streets. They look different. Unrecognisable. No landmarks correspond with my internal map. I can't be certain what's road and what's sidewalk except where there are markers. The signs are all covered in frost. I drive up and down what should be Heather's street but can't identify her house. I turn the corner and drive the next parallel street, and the next, but they look foreign to me.

The children are getting restless, so I pass back the tray of cheesy muffins I rose early this morning to bake. My penance for the few hours of social time I crave. Dawn starts crying. She's probably hungry. But stopping anywhere along the street in these conditions seems like a death wish. It would be wiser to wait until we pass a shopping mall or a gas station and park where the snow has been ploughed from the tarmac. What if I get bogged? We have one of those ice shovel-scraper tools on board but I've so far avoided using one. There are hardly any other vehicles on the road. I wonder, will I be the only one stupid enough to drive to mothers' group with an infant and three small children?

Finally, I admit I'm lost beyond comprehension. Dawn's cries bring on a let-down which adds to my confusion. Feeding her is now a matter of urgency. The windscreen wipers are getting icy and I need to stop and check an actual map before I drive us clear across the New Hampshire border.

I see a widening of the road outside a house with a high surrounding wall. It looks like a private, sheltered place to stop. I could park there for ten minutes with the engine running and climb into the back of our SUV to study the map and feed Dawn. I commit. Turn the wheel, brake and pull over.

But the car doesn't respond. The wall's coming at us. The ABS brakes shudder, but the wall's still upon us. I brace for impact. Unsecured objects, toys and bags, surge frontward. The car rattles to a stop just inches from the wall. I look over my shoulder at the children holding their muffins. Wide-eyed, they stare back at me.

Elijah announces, 'That was fun!'

I grip the wheel and breathe deep. The road looked deceptively flat and white. Maybe I hit a patch of frozen puddle obscured by snow. The dreaded black ice.

'We all good?' I ask, winded. 'Everyone safe?' My heart is trying to escape my chest. Even Dawn's howling has stopped. Thank you, modern braking systems! I grab the map and with a shaky finger, trace my route, figuring out where I am and how far to the closest homeward exit. I put the car into gear, ease my foot on the pedal and drive.

Once home, I settle into the rocking chair in our bedroom and give Dawn her catch-up feed. I rock back and forth reflecting on what happened. I'm an idiot to let loneliness overshadow my family's safety. We could have had a tragic accident. Tears begin and I wipe them away but now the dam has breached, and I begin to sniffle and sob an uncontrolled ugly cry. My shoulders bounce with the effort of holding back all the tension and the sound coming from me could wake the dead. Dawn pauses her feeding to look up at me.

The children enter the room. Their little faces drawn with worry, all three.

'Mummy, what's wrong?' asks Elijah.

I try to muster my dignity, but my inner child feels abandoned and I can't be the parent right now.

'Mummy feels sad. I miss my friends. I'm lonely.'

Ruby puts her little hand on my arm, 'Don't worry Mum, we're your friends.' The wisdom of a four-year-old. 'Would you like a tissue?'

'Yes, please,' I blubber.

'I'll get you some water, Mum,' Elijah is already reaching for the glass on my bedside table. My Munchkins deliver tissues and life-sustaining water.

Kyle tries to make me smile, 'Mummy, poo, baby!'

February 2006

Nancy forwards an email to me, about a midwifery conference in Boston, and the theme is *Mother-Friendly Childbirth: Closing the Gap between Research and Practice*. Anxious to keep my hand in maternity matters, I purchase a two-day pass, expecting to attend with Dawn in her baby carrier. It'll be difficult, but I figure, from being among midwives all these years, that no one will object to a baby in the room.

I take a seat at the back for the first lecture, so I can discreetly escape if Dawn makes a fuss. I expect other mothers and babies will join me, but as the attendees fill the room, it appears Dawn and I are the one and only. I shouldn't have assumed that consumers would be welcome. Maybe they don't have the growing culture of consumer consultation we've cultivated in Australia.

The keynote speaker, Dr Christiane Northrup, presents *Birth: The Foundation of Mother-Daughter Wisdom*. I'm moved by her story, how she lost a section of her breast to a complication from mastitis, because she couldn't balance pumping milk with the urgency of her hospital role.

On day two, I attend the renowned pregnancy and childbirth author, Henci Goer's, presentation of the clinical and social evidence behind The *Mother-Friendly Childbirth Initiative*. Afterwards, she seeks me out, as the only person with a baby in the room. Upon hearing my accent, she breaks into a smile, 'I'll be in Australia next week!' One week from now, Jo Smethurst will email a picture from Australia, and Henci will be front and centre, attending a pizza party at Bruce's house with all of my Brisbane friends.

In the afternoon, we break into self-assigned discussion groups. I choose *It Takes a Village: Implementing Change Through Community Coalitions and Task Forces*. The kindly midwife next to me offers to hold Dawn so I can take a break. In our group is founder and editor of *Midwifery Today*, Jan Tritten.

She says, 'The medical lobby's so powerful that people don't understand what midwives do. Wouldn't it be great to buy every billboard along the I-90, presenting their local midwife, until we saturate America with normal birth? Maybe some of you don't know, but homebirth is still illegal in some states.'

'What about you, Australia?' she gestures toward me. 'Tell us what's happening where you're from.'

I point at my chest with a questioning look and she nods. So, I explain about the network of maternity consumer groups in

Australia, collaborating to get consumer representation legislated for all hospital and health policy committees.

There isn't enough time to tell the stories; how maternity consumers staged Airing Our Laundry, the Waterbirth Rally, and acquired a promise of a Birth Centre, with more in the pipeline. It occurs to me that, in my tiny corner of the globe at least, thoughtful and committed citizens did make a small difference. The challenge will be to keep it.

Late April 2006

Sad news comes via the network. A Queensland woman lost her baby giving birth on the roadside. Her local hospital in Emerald wouldn't admit her, because they had no maternity staff. They'd advised that she drive to Rockhampton, whose hospital, with neonatal intensive care, was over three hours away. It highlights the issue of skill loss in remote communities, that they couldn't make an exception for a woman in active labour. And so, maternity wards continue to close even though women keep having babies.

What went wrong for them, beyond the obvious pressure to travel? I torture myself wondering was it a boy or girl child? Did she have other children? I recall Tamara and the baby that died at the Birth Centre, and the family we never learned about. And even Kath's baby Christian comes to mind. How does a new mother cope with the heartache once her womb is empty but there's no baby to nurture? Hormones will do what they do, regardless.

For distraction, I compulsively check my email. Kareena has sent pictures of our house-in-progress, bless her. I miss her. I scroll through the picture roll and marvel at the bare bone's construction, wondering which room I'm looking at, or through. Then my email pings. An unexpected familiar name appears. Why would Claudia, an old classmate, make contact? We met briefly at the school reunion a few years ago but have honestly been out of contact for eighteen years. If she's in Australia, she's up at three in the morning.

I click my mouse. The email opens to a casual greeting.

Hello Jodie.

I found some old notes from high school and have been wondering whether to reach out to you. Finally decided, why not? How's life? Where are you now? I heard you're living abroad. Thanks for organising the reunion. I'm sorry we didn't get to talk much that night, but it was nice to see everyone again.

Regards, Claudia.

I pause and let this information compute. Claudia and I did senior subjects together in high school but went off to separate universities. We were acquainted, but I wouldn't say we were close. She was a conscientious student, a good listener and, as I got to know her, a kind friend.

She was a disciplined person then, smarter than me, and her family had high expectations. She couldn't know how years later; her influence would prompt me to adopt a writing practice that enabled my own evolution and growth. It still does.

More than a few times, she'd tutored me in the mathematics concepts I failed to grasp, with a patience and kindness that I never reciprocated. How did I miss connecting with her at the reunion?

I devise my response to her email out of curiosity and maybe a sniff of nostalgia. With the children occupied, I rest my fingers on the keyboard and type.

Claudia,

What a surprise! Thank you for that trip down memory lane. I'm sorry I missed you at the reunion too, there's so much for us to catch up on. I never used the maths we did ever again. Honestly, couldn't have pursued it further and hated it by the end. What keeps you busy these days?

Jodie

I walk away from the computer expecting a response will take days. But within a minute my laptop pings. What follows is a protracted email exchange which, if we'd been in the same room or on the telephone, might transpire to be a conversation like this:

I suppose you remember Paul. Would you believe we're married now? With four children? The youngest is two months old.

Claudia and I corresponded briefly in the first year of university. She knew I was in the first rocky year of a relationship, and then we fell out of contact. When she saw me at the reunion with my enormous belly, we didn't talk about family. In fact, we barely talked at all.

We're in Massachusetts, a world away from Brisbane. Our family is complete and now I'm just swimming in kid stuff.

That's wonderful. I'm happy for you.

Yet, there's a wistful tone to her response. I check the children are all safely engaged in play and settle at my laptop.

It's the middle of the day here. If you're in Australia then it's like, 3.30 am! What's keeping you up tonight?

Immediately, I regret my question. Is it any of my business?

Jodie, it's been a crappy year. The hardest year of my life. I don't sleep. I suppose I'm reaching out to tell you how we're connected beyond matrices and vectors.

We are?

When I found your notes among mine, I decided to look you up. Your name and email are on the website for Friends of the Birth Centre and I saw you wrote some letters in The Courier-Mail. You've been busy.

I reply. *I'm so sorry you're having a crappy year.*

I've been following your work, especially since I had a baby at the Birth Centre. With Tamara.

Her words circuit my head before they land, and I re-read them to be certain. The penny drops. My fingers tremble at the keyboard. This can't be real.

Claudia, are you telling me...?

How do I proceed without confirmation?

...that it was your baby, last year at the Birth Centre?

It was.

I sit back in my chair and pull my hands from the keyboard. My heart pounds in my chest so hard I can see it through my shirt. I can't leave the conversation now, not that I want to, but I know that no response I offer will be adequate.

I don't know what to say...I'm so sorry I didn't know names.

I wipe my eyes and smooth my face and appear calm for the sake of the children.

It's alright, I understand. It was just hard to read your Letters to the Editor when Mary-Rose's Birth Wars feature was published, and after the 'Killing Fields' debacle on TV. Life hasn't been the same. My husband and I haven't recovered. We've struggled with infertility and of course our baby was desperately wanted. I doubt we'll have another. And so, I wondered if you'd like to know her name. Because, in all of this, though she only lived for a couple of hours, she was a person. Her name was Persephone.

I read her reply and inhale it. Such a pretty name. She would be almost two years old, if circumstances were different. A toddler, walking and talking and brimming with personality. I need a moment to collect myself. I swallow the lump in my throat and look at my own babies, blurred through tears, playing in the next room, oblivious to the fragile web of life. Their conception, gestation and birth, taken for granted.

Her name was Persephone.

I have trouble falling asleep that night. When I do it isn't restful. In my nightmare, I'm in front of Brisbane's City Hall, in King George Square, at some grand happening, an amalgamation of all our rallies and events. I sit down on some grass to play with Dawn. I look away, and suddenly, she's gone. I search but can't find her in the crowd. One minute she was in my arms, and then she wasn't. I'm all empty arms, a hollow heart and bottomless misery. I wake in a cold panic. I gather my wits and get my bearings. Dawn sleeps beside me, warm and safe. Paul lies on the other side, his breathing deep and raspy. I stare at the ceiling for I don't know how long, wishing things could have been different, for Claudia, for Tamara, for everyone.

Most of all, for Persephone.

39 A TURF WAR

Early May 2006

My misery and guilt over Claudia's baby coincide with the launch of the Gold Coast Birth Centre. While I'd always understood there would have been extraordinary pain and loss after Persephone, whose name I'd never known, I'd focussed on the evidence that supports Birth Centres and midwifery care. But I'd walled off the reality of one couple's loss. A couple I now know by name, with whom I share personal history.

Advocates aren't supposed to get caught up in the individual stories. Public servants can smell counter-productive emotionality at twenty paces. Statistics are the tools in trade. They communicate facts and remove the extraneous emotion. We're supposed to quote means and averages that can never represent individual stories or the events that make them extraordinary. Data can't measure sleepless nights, unanswered questions, and aching grief.

Statistics don't have names that get embedded in your psyche. They roll off the tongue, unlike the stories behind them. I hate statistics now. I've been taking them for granted.

The network is abuzz. Enough researchers reviewing the *Term Breech Trial* criticised the study's design, methods, and conclusions to have the findings retracted. No outcome is still an outcome, meaning they couldn't identify whether one mode of birth or the other is better for babies. The study just wasn't viable. A properly rigorous study would be unethical, removing women's civil liberties and randomly allocating birth choices will never come to pass. Only through detailed retrospective studies may we ever know more.

We can't bring back the past six years. In that time, we have a new generation of interns and midwives who've never witnessed a breech birth. Whenever will they get to assist one? Why ever would they start now? Fear of litigation allows hospitals to apply flawed evidence to justify their policies. It's got nothing to do with what's best for women and babies. The State pays hospitals for performing surgery, not avoiding it. That means, in maternity care, it's caesareans that pay the bills.

Melissa Fox, our spokeswoman for waterbirth, is representing consumers at the Mater Mothers' Hospital, liaising on the development of a Midwifery Group Practice. She has just announced her second pregnancy and, like so many of us, is opting out of the system and hiring a midwife in private practice. The insurance situation means that midwives attend births at home at calculated risk to their financial security. Litigation is unlikely when a pregnant client is making informed decisions about her care.

Natural Parenting continues to grow in membership, but it's a more volatile place than it used to be. Janet's influence is strong, and her network is wide. Dozens of similarly passionate feminists from all over Australia, and the world, are joining our little forum and changing the flavour of our interactions. Debates flare daily. Timid members have fled to the more soothing cloth nappy and breastfeeding sites. Discussion tiptoes around pregnancy and birth in the face of strong recommendations from Janet's colleagues to homebirth, or free birth without a midwife.

Suspicion of midwives is unfounded in my experience – they make the well-being of mother and baby the locus of their care – but with a growing community of women proselytising about unhindered birth, and the power of the female, I rarely dip my toe in the debates these days.

Keen to repair public trust in Queensland Health following the Bundaberg scandal, Premier Peter Beattie continues his mission to upgrade regional hospitals. Anticipating this year's election campaign, and receptive to Philippa Scott's active lobbying, he promises to fund a Birth Centre for Townsville in north Queensland.

November 2006

Another Halloween passes. A bitter winter is about to begin in Massachusetts and our home-born baby is turning one. After Christmas, we'll return to Australia, and our newly completed house, so Elijah and Ruby can start at the local public school. I'm keen to re-engage with family and friends. This has been a year of firsts for all of us – first white Christmas, Fourth of July, and all the traditions of our host country. We're surrounded by apple orchards and cranberry ponds, literary history and graveyards hundreds of years old where the American forefathers are buried. I wonder about the 'foremothers' too. I'll miss the deep history here.

I'm still attending mothers' groups with Nancy and Heather, different as they are. Many in Heather's group are kind and welcoming women who follow Christian Science which, I confess, is foreign to me. Nancy's circle is wide and diverse. The people who come are endlessly interesting. I arrive at her door, and see a new picture in the glass, the one Nancy took of me with the children, my belly exposed to the cool autumn air.

Today, a young traditional midwife tells us about birth customs in Hawaii, and I learn that the tradition of planting a tree with the placenta originated there, perhaps in other cultures too. On no account is the tree to be cut down while the child is alive. I never thought about appropriating Hawaiian customs as a bad thing. It was only ever a meaningful way to process my experience and welcome my baby home.

I give Nancy a signed copy of Sarah Buckley's first edition, *Gentle Birth, Gentle Mothering*, for her lending library. Nancy tells me she wrote a book called *Silent Knife*, and that she'd like to write another. She introduces me to another writer. Her name is Raquel and I find her aura magnetic. She's a lawyer, stirred to action after a traumatic birth. Oh, the stereotypes in my head!

I don't expect her to be so fragile, soft-spoken and empathetic. She recounts her experience of Post-Traumatic Stress with the broken familiarity of the many stories I've heard before. She says she has a story to tell, but she doesn't know where to start.

I offer my unsolicited, and somewhat obvious, advice.

'Start at the moment that changed everything.'

'What do you mean?'

'Your caesarean.'

'Oh, you mean...' She drains of colour.

'Write about your surgery.' Did I really say it aloud to someone with PTSD? The poor woman is traumatised enough.

I take my leave, pack myself and the kids and all their stuff in the car. I just couldn't shut my mouth, could I?

A few weeks later, Nancy calls.

'You know Raquel has been writing furiously since she met you.'

'I was worried I'd upset her.'

'Whatever you said, it worked,' says Nancy with her usual exuberance. 'She's writing and it's good!'

'That's fantastic!' Thank the universe I didn't traumatise her.

'So, we want you to join us. Let's all write our books and change the face of birth.'

'I think my story's dull. It's all much too happy.'

'Oh Jodie! The happy stories give us hope. The world needs hope.'

January 2007

Exhausted. Jet lagged. We've left the icy winds of Massachusetts and returned to the sub-tropical blast of midsummer Brisbane. We arrive at our new home late at night with a child no one has met beyond pictures on a website.

Magically, there's bread and milk in the fridge, rice and pasta in the pantry. There's even a home-made dinner we can reheat. Our friends have ensured we'll feel welcome. And we do. The hot mince pie and curried pea and potato taste better than any take away meal. How did they make this happen? Kareena must have obtained a key.

We've finally overcome our jet lag, but it's taken more than a week, with the children up at all hours of the day and night. Mum and I have spoken only occasionally over the past two years. She's battling depression, attempting to manage it with medication that causes unpleasant side-effects. She's stopped driving and doesn't want to leave the house. I don't hesitate to pick up the phone.

'Mum, can we come visit?'

'When? All of you? Here?'

There's tension in her voice. It seems she'd rather we didn't visit, but since she hasn't met her granddaughter, I stand firm. Paul has returned to the US, to wrap up the final two months of his contract. The separation will be tough. I'm on Mum's doorstep within two days.

It's never easy travelling with the children, poor sleepers as they are. It taxes my personal reserves, since I get so little sleep. It's also difficult for those around us who are not accustomed to the noise and chaos. Something inevitably gets broken, there's unavoidable loud noise and commotion, and the constant requirement for me to feed, toilet and clean up after them.

My mother, who always loved being with her grandchildren, seems overwhelmed and fearful: of the neighbours, of the high schoolers who walk past her gate. She worries that her sleeplessness disturbs us at night. I try my best to reassure her, but the script in her head is louder. I struggle to understand the changes in her and am out of my depth. Her pain is palpable, preventing her from functioning, and there's no room in it for me. For any of us. I stand at the gate of my mother's isolation with no key for access. We speak as if across a void.

'Please, Jodie, can you turn the TV down? I can't stand the noise.'

'Quiet down everyone, the neighbours aren't used to having children around.'

'Stay away from the road!'

'Careful on the stairs!'

'Are they safe in the bath?'

'I'm so sorry...for all the pain I've caused.'

I want to hug her, but don't know if she wants me to, so I pat her arm. 'I'm sorry too, Mum. It'll be all right.' I don't know what else to say so I add, 'I love you.'

That night after dinner, with the children in bed, we sit at her table and open the bottle of Chianti that's been sitting in

Mum's fridge for months. She never was one to drink, and never more than two glasses. I pour her a half-glass, hoping she'll relax and maybe sleep a little easier. I pour a full one for myself because, dammit, today was hard. We sit in exhausted silence until I speak.

'Are you okay, Mum?'

'I'm just settling in with this medication. It doesn't leave me feeling very well. The doctor says it takes two months to resolve, so I have to wait it out.'

Before tonight, I'd blamed Mum for busting up our family, for choosing the most damaging and hurtful time to leave, and for punishing us with her silence. Now I can see that she was a woman on a sinking ship. She had to rescue herself, cling to whatever flotsam would keep her from drowning. And she's still swimming for her life, caught in a rip tide that's pulling her further and further from the shore.

I hope, for her sake, the medication works. I hope that balance will return. That her laugh will return. That her energy will return. That she'll return to us.

I miss her.

40 TRANSITION

November 2007

I look down and notice two-year-old Dawn is still wearing her training pants. Ergo: she's dry. I realise we have an opportunity but the usual suggestion of, 'Potty?' is met with an adamant shake of the head. Never mind. There's always later. I turn on the stereo and select some music.

She asks for her cup of milk, which I retrieve from the fridge. She gulps to quench a thirst I failed to anticipate and, tuning into the beat, she bops and skips then pushes her little face upwards, lips pursed for a milky kiss. I adore you.

Bend down, kiss and spin. With an element of stealth, I steer my little groover towards the bathroom. She responds to the unspoken suggestion, dances off her undies, and climbs on her seat for the big toilet with a bop, bop, weeee! Relief glazes her face.

I point my fingers and disco dance where she sits with knickers around her ankles and we savour a moment of unhurried connection. When done, I dress her, and we wash our hands. In my prior life, I would never have attributed opportunities for loving and nurturing to a potty trip, but I'm wiser now. There's exquisite beauty in the mundane.

We return to the living room where Paul and Elijah are negotiating the appropriate number of hours for a seven-year-old to play computer games. I lean down and audibly whisper to Ruby, 'Dawn did a wee in the big toilet.'

The girls lock eyes. Big sister winks and gives a thumbs up. Dawn responds with a nod and point. Savvy beyond her years.

I sense the beginning of the end. She looks less like my baby every day.

'What a big girl!' I say. 'Let's call Nana. She'll be so proud of you!'

Earlier this year, Maternity Coalition's National President, Justine Caines, and Bruce, as Vice-President, met the talented Shadow Minister for Health and Aging, Nicola Roxon, accompanied by representatives: Leslie Arnott from Victoria and Kelley Stewart, a local constituent. Their ambitious agenda: Medicare for midwives. Everyone says a win for Labor's Kevin Rudd could pave the way for extensive national health reforms. According to Bruce, Ms Roxon asked, 'What can I give you without giving you Medicare?' Justine was so vexed, she left Roxon's office and resigned from Maternity Coalition, forthwith. She started her own party, called What Women Want, to represent key issues for women, like paid maternity leave, childcare, post-natal services, education and environmental protections to safeguard our children's future.

Meanwhile, Peter Beattie retires as Queensland Premier. The popular former treasurer, Anna Bligh, succeeds him. With the Townsville Birth Centre construction wrapping up, Liz Wilkes attempts to secure a Birth Centre for Toowoomba, too. She forms Friends of the Birth Centre Darling Downs, and they exploit their media contacts to successfully ambush the Premier on her press circuit. Confronted by a gathering of women in an inflatable birth pool, Anna Bligh demands, 'How did you know I would be here?'

It was an inside job. They don't secure a Birth Centre for Toowoomba in this round.

September 2007

Bruce takes me to meet Julia Gillard, Kevin Rudd's loyal deputy, on her Federal leadership campaign trail. She seems to know about the conversations between Nicola Roxon and Maternity Coalition and says she supports a more collaborative arrangement between midwives, GPs and obstetricians. I switch Dawn to my other hip to shake her hand, but I don't get the sense the issue is important to her personally. Her star is rising. Maybe she'll be Prime Minister one day.

Late November 2007

Kevin Rudd is declared the 26th Prime Minister of Australia. He takes the stage to rousing applause and delivers his election speech flanked by his family.

What Women Want didn't put a great dent in the preferences of Mr and Mrs Average, but what's important is that they represented a women's agenda and got a larger than previous slice of the Federal pie. WWW allocated preferences to the Greens, who've always supported in-home health care, reproductive rights for women, and homebirth. And of course, the Green Party preferences flow to Labor, contributing to their landslide victory.

A few months from now, Prime Minister Kevin Rudd will sign the Kyoto Protocol for Climate Change and televise his apology to Indigenous Australia and the Stolen Generations. He'll withdraw our remaining troops from combat in Iraq and release an economic stimulus package to cushion Australia's economy through the Global Financial Crisis. For a while at least, Kevin

Rudd's leadership represents a golden hope for Maternity Coalition. Federal maternity reform is feeling like a realistic and achievable goal.

December 2007

The *Natural Parenting* forum is imploding. Advertising is introduced to the previously neutral space and members don't receive the content well. Janet's own forum, called *Joyous Birth*, is now well-established. Articulate, funny, passionate women have left our community in droves.

I register a login and browse the discussions, but I don't know how to engage with the discussion on *Joyous Birth*. I find big personalities, radical feminism and liberal political debate where the discourse quotes Alice in *Through The Looking Glass*, 'curiouser and curiouser!' and anyone using the word 'lady' will discover the word mysteriously converts to 'woman'. The atmosphere makes me anxious in the pit of my stomach. But with *Natural Parenting* no more, where do I belong?

May 2008

It pours with rain the day the Mater reveals its newly constructed Mater Mothers hospital with a new and improved Midwifery Group Practice. Melissa Fox formed relationships with decision-makers developing the MGP, and she gets an honorary role in the opening ceremonies wearing her home born baby on her back. Later, we all get to tour the new maternity wing. It's validating to see a hospital celebrate its consumer representatives this way.

October 2008

Last night's love making was really something else. There's hope for my sorry libido yet. I shrug off my dressing gown and run the hot water.

The children are dressed. School lunches are made. I've ten minutes before we must all be in the car to go. Time enough for a quick shower. I might once have resented the meagre ten minutes, but today it's all I need.

Lathering with soap, I discover a glob of mucous as clear as the white of a fresh chicken's egg. I feel a rush of adrenaline. Shit! I could have sworn I'm still a few days off fertile.

I turn off the water and reach for a towel. Between dressing and brushing my teeth, I wipe the steamy mirror. My reflection frowns at me. I rub my brow with the fingers of my free hand, but the furrows are deep and persistent.

I go through the motions of the day, driving the kids around, doing my errands, and starting on dinner, but my mind is a dog with a bone. When Paul gets home, I can't give him the welcome I've been practising.

'Christ, what a day! I don't think it could have gone worse to tell the truth, but it sure is good to come home to you.' He plants a kiss on my cheek. His eyes communicate that he's savouring the memory of last night.

'How're you feeling?' He takes a beer from the fridge. The lid hisses as he twists it off and puts the bottle to his lips.

'I'm okay.'

'Really? You don't look it.'

'Well,' I blurt, 'this morning in the shower, I had a slick of mucous.'

He has another sip of beer. Comprehension doesn't immediately register in his face, so I translate, 'You know, ovulation...'

Paul blanches and doubles over the kitchen bench, exhaling as if I've slugged his stomach with more strength than I possess.

'You've got to be kidding me.'

We stand in uncomfortable silence for I don't know how long.

This is not the reaction I expected. I know he's crazy busy at work, juggling roles, preparing to travel again next week, and with a big government contract on the table...this isn't good timing. I watch him take three swigs of beer in a row, leaving the bottle half empty.

'I shouldn't have told you. It's not a sure thing.'

'How soon can we know?'

'In about two weeks.'

He shakes his head, like this is unacceptable.

'I'm away late next week. I need to know the odds. What's the chance that you're...' he licks his lips like his mouth is too dry to utter the word, 'pregnant? Ten percent? Twenty?'

I stiffen, remembering that night in his mother's kitchen ten years ago, when he insisted, we start a family.

'How can I estimate it?' I put my fingers to my temples, a high-pitched ringing in my ears.

'I'm just telling you I'm having fertile signs and that last night was...' my voice trails off.

'You're telling me!' He leans on his elbows, at the kitchen bench, palms to face. Then he stands up and challenges me, 'You did this on purpose!'

My mouth falls open. 'No! And I can't believe you said that!' I turn away with tears in my eyes. How did this become all my fault?

Dinner is burned but I serve it anyway. We sit together at the table in the usual chaos. The children are making jokes and loudly talking nonsense, but a bubble of silence hangs between Paul and me. I have visions of enduring another pregnancy and birth, another year and beyond of breastfeeding. I feel tired and overwhelmed, pulled out of shape every single day, like I don't have, or can't provide, everything the children need to become healthy, confident, functional human beings. Mother guilt weighs heavy on my shoulder.

The children draw my attention back to the table, here and now. Elijah's asking for seconds. Ruby's laughing with an open mouthful of food. Kyle's running around and around the table in circles, while Dawn eats her food with her fingers, using her hair for a napkin.

Paul's face rests in his hands. Dinner untouched. A second bottle of beer sits empty in front of him. We corral the children towards the television to give ourselves space to talk.

Beer number three is open and on the bench. I reach over, pick it up and take a swig for myself.

We calculate that, if I am pregnant, I'll be midway through the first trimester when he does his longest business trip of the year. His mother lives with us now – deteriorating in health and needing daily assistance. The children's school routine keeps me hustling, plus chasing an active toddler. I'm back at Friends of the Birth Centre, which is in a different place now. With the permanence of the Birth Centre guaranteed, membership has shrunk from over 400 families back to prior numbers. I'm presenting around Brisbane at the *Where To Have Your Baby* seminars for the Childbirth Education Association. How will I hold things together?

A week later, I answer the phone to Paul's sister, Kay.

'Are you all right?'

'Yeeess, why?'

'I talked to Paul on the weekend. He seemed stressed. I just wondered...is your marriage okay?'

We've watched Kay raise a child as a single mother after her first marriage dissolved. We've seen her happily remarry and raise two more beautiful babies, then nurse her husband through the most harrowing of cancers and grieve through the loneliness that followed. Yet, she picked herself up and carried on with grace. I decide to own it.

'We've had a pregnancy scare.'

'Oh,' she says with relief, 'is that all?'

'Is that all?' I choke. 'We've had the most awful time, Kay. Paul isn't talking to me.'

She waits a few beats. 'Jodie, you two are bigger than this. It's not the end of the world. You have four beautiful, beautiful children. What's one more? You'll cope. You always have.'

In a moment's insight, I see the ridiculousness, and smile. We're perfectly capable of raising another child. We'll be fine. The kids will be fine. It's not what we planned, but there are plenty of worse things that could happen. We all have our health, and that's enormous.

The next day, Paul takes himself off for a vasectomy. When my period arrives It's a double blow. No baby now. No more babies ever.

41 AFTERBIRTH

February 2009

Everyone's talking about Facebook, and so far, I've resisted. But I decide to register and gingerly search for people, old school friends, extended family and names in my local community.

I've been feeling adrift since the collapse of the *Natural Parenting* forum. Mothering is different now the kids are in school. Dawn is in kindergarten, but I still have questions, or need support, from like-minded parents sometimes. I miss my tribe. I search the names of some forum friends. Et voila! Here they are, almost all of them. Many have now made new careers as nurses and midwives, teachers and writers. There are even a few politicians! It's fascinating how having children can shift the focus of your life.

Improving Maternity Services in Australia is the report of the Federal Maternity Services Review. It acknowledges the role of informed consumer influence in maternity care policy and recommends that maternity care in public hospitals reduce their dependence on high-tech specialist services and embrace midwife-led maternity care. It has all the right rhetoric, but the AMA will inevitably push back on this like they've done before.

April 2009

My mobile phone rings.

'Jodie,' I recognise my friend's voice. There's an urgency in her tone.

'Angie! What's the matter?'

'It's awful. Are you sitting down? Janet's baby died.'

I knew that Janet from the *Natural Parenting* forum, who left to form *Joyous Birth*, was pregnant a third time. She'd been planning a very public free birth after finding it difficult to secure a midwife. I also knew her dear friend Olivia, who brought the eyebright tea, intended to be her birth support.

'What? When...how?'

'I don't know. I saw a post, but it's gone now. Deleted.'

'Oh Angie...what can I say?'

Janet had openly promoted free birth. It's not something I advocate, but it's something I understand. I wasn't present in the room, so I'm not entitled to speculate about what, if anything, went wrong. No one who chooses to free birth is choosing a dead baby.

'And you know what's weird about it?' Angie sounds on the verge of crying. 'The forum's so quiet. It's eerie.'

'Why'd you call me, Ang?' She knows I'm not a fan of *Joyous Birth*.

'Because I know you care, Jodie.'

I do care. But I'm no one. I'm devastated for Janet, and her family, of course I am. There can be no intellectual or political argument about it. Just compassion for a mother's grief. She'll be vilified by the media and the public. This won't end well for her.

May 2009

Liz Wilkes and her team of advocates, women and babies, greet Premier Anna Bligh in Toowoomba, more formally this time, and receive a promise of a Birth Centre the next day. Together with the Australian College of Midwives, Liz has been instrumental in getting the federal health bean counters to promise Medicare funding for midwives and, hopefully, an insurance solution. Progress is slow but steady.

The federal government releases the health budget. It has taken four years, but a recommendation of the *Rebirthing* report has come to fruition. Queensland establishes the Centre for Mothers and Babies at the University of Queensland to integrate an evidence-based consumer focus for maternity care. Nationally, thanks to the scandal in Bundaberg, they propose a single registration body should regulate all health services, across all States in Australia. The Australian Health Practitioner Regulations Agency, or AHPRA, is intended to prevent dodgy practitioners from moving interstate to evade discipline for poor performance. Midwives will have to demonstrate 'eligibility' via a national registration and accreditation scheme. Ostensibly, these new organisations will allow their predecessors to be dissolved and a new culture to emerge that empowers, and consults with, consumers.

September 2009

I'm attending the National Day of Action at a community hall in Bardon on behalf of Friends of the Birth Centre, probably for the last time. All told there are around 60 midwives and advocates in the room with their children. Liz Wilkes wears her toddler in a sling. Jenny Gamble and Jocelyn Toohill have stepped into roles with more influence on the next generation of midwives, and the policy impacting them. Melissa Fox and Jo Smethurst are here, too.

An organiser welcomes us, advising that the paper scroll around three walls of the room denotes a timeline of Queensland birth reform from 1992 until 2009. We're invited to take a marker and write our memories on the timeline. Mothers, midwives and advocates come forward to add their stories, passing the markers back and forth until we can stand back and observe the history of our campaign spread over three walls. From the instability of the 1990s, when Birth Centres were opened and closed in a short cycle, to investigations and reviews and their subsequent reports recommending reforms to maternity care, such as *Options for Effective Care in Childbirth, Rocking The Cradle*, and *Rebirthing.* It also documents the installation of tubs at the Royal and other hospitals, NMAP, and the medical indemnity crisis, closures to regional birthing services, the formation of Birthtalk, the FBC events, and more.

Bruce stands on the dais, ready to speak to the crowd about the newly announced reforms. We're not sure how to interpret the changes.

What's clear is midwives can have Medicare provider numbers and access to the Pharmaceutical Benefits Scheme, paving a road to self-employment again. Obstacles to visiting rights in hospitals have been removed for eligible midwives and the process of hiring a private midwife for antenatal care in the home should be quite straightforward. So far, so good, but there are conditions, which are disappointing, but expected. For example, birth is restricted to hospital. Without a major shift in culture, the power relationship still falls in the direction of obstetrics. So, why should the culture of providing maternity care change?

What isn't clear is whether there's any hope of an indemnity insurance solution that will enable midwives in private practice to attend birth at home. Nicola Roxon says to subsidise an insurance package is unviable. An exemption from requiring insurance has been granted, but for how long? Women aren't going to wait around for birth to reform itself. Babies come when babies come, and women compelled to have their babies at home will continue to make that choice, with or without a midwife.

Our collective sadness at the shortcomings of these reforms means the homebirth rally in Canberra is inevitable.

The 'mother of all rallies' disrupts Qantas flights to Canberra, bumping a number of mothers and babies from their nominated seats; something about policies regarding the maximum number of infants permitted on a single flight, or possibly a shortage of baby seat belts (what little use they are). But my friends and I still make it to the Indigenous Tent Embassy in time for the Welcome To Country that inaugurates the rally.

We form a large circle around the fire. The smoking ceremony is led by Wiradjuri elder, Isobel Coe, and Indigenous birth advocate, Fleur Magick. I'm moved to witness this display in the company of my women-friends. I wipe tears from my eyes. Then someone behind me hisses, 'What the hell is *she* doing here?'

I turn to look but the voice doesn't belong to anyone I know. I lean toward Angie and ask, 'Who's she talking about?'

'I think she means Lisa Barrett,' she says, 'the woman with dreadlocks beside the welcome party.

'She's a midwife from Adelaide. Attends homebirths other midwives won't touch. About a month ago, a baby died. Apparently, breech.'

By all reports, Lisa Barrett is an experienced and qualified midwife, willing to support women's choices beyond the comfort zone of some. In Australia's birth climate, if a woman feels backed into a corner and unable to negotiate with maternal health services, she'll seek out a midwife like Lisa, who will give her what she wants. Or she'll opt for no birth support at all. They're a minority. But everyone attending this rally is a minority – several thousand of us who support homebirth.

When the time comes to march to the green, where the rally will be held, I unravel the Friends of the Birth Centre banner and convince a few others to help me carry it. Bruce and so many others were right, I can see that now. If we don't make provisions for private midwives with legitimate, affordable insurance, then midwives like Lisa Barrett will be the only ones working in the homebirth space.

By the time we get to the green I'm far from the stage and my view is obscured by signs and banners and women much taller than me. Banners declare, *My Baby, My Body, My Way* and *I want my birth: not your options and Women of the Earth, Take Back Your Birth.*

Justine Caines, from What Women Want, wears a purple t-shirt declaring '*Home Birth Rocks*' – her belly just prominent enough to identify her eighth pregnancy. When I catch a peek of the stage, I see hundreds of purple outlines of a pregnant person on wire stakes in the grass. Each bears a picture or a name, a virtual presence at the rally for women who couldn't travel but wanted their support recognised today.

Speakers on the stage receive the rapt support of the crowd, including the Honourable Peter Dutton, of the House of Representatives, Shadow Minister for Health and Aging, not that we'll ever hear him speak about homebirth again.

The children are all in school now, and Dawn goes to half-day pre-school. Ah, the luxury of a hot shower. Alone. With the door open. The water's so hot it fogs the mirror. I exhale and put my face into the stream. A waterfall runs over my head and neck, lather runs in waves and rivers down the geography of my body. It has been months since I've had an unrushed moment to myself. I dry myself, shoulders, face, hair.

The mirror reports the lines of my face, and a new droop in my body. My hair is salt and pepper. Nine years of intensive child-raising has etched dark circles under my eyes, and lines at the outer corners betray almost four decades under the harsh Australian sun.

Dimples pockmark the translucent skin of my thighs, and the fur I allow to grow on my legs and underarms feels normal to me now. My belly has shiny white lines and loose skin below my navel that becomes an apron when I bend over. Pregnancy and breastfeeding have left my breasts hollow and formless. Unseeable parts of me sag too. I must check myself before I sneeze or cough or laugh.

I brought four children into this world and I worry for their future. For our global climate. For their access to the levelling benefits of public health care, education, and social services. I hope their births will matter. I feel satisfaction, watching them grow and develop independence. I'm loving the anticipation of what comes next – when they'll bathe and dress and organise their learning materials without me. When they'll manage their own feeding and toileting and sleep. What will happen to their mother when they no longer need me? I feel myself on the cusp of change. Like a chrysalis waiting to transform. I'll emerge and display my true form to the world.

42 THE FOURTH TRIMESTER

March 2019

Ten years on, I drive to visit Bruce and Erika at Mt Glorious. I park my car where I'm told and walk down their rocky driveway to their beautiful bespoke home.

Bruce wears a torn work shirt and greets me, just like old times.

'You dressed up!' We laugh and take stock of each other.

'Has it really been ten years since we've seen you?' Bruce scratches his head in thought. 'No, there was the twentieth anniversary of the Birth Centre in 2015.'

'I waited for the big storm to pass and the party was over when I arrived.'

Bruce invites me to cross the threshold. The house is unchanged, except for a new wood heater installed right where Erika's birth pool once stood. The mistress of the house emerges from the kitchen to greet me. They have a little more silver in their hair, but their faces are as I remember. Erika asks me about the children, though they're not children anymore.

Elijah is nineteen, driving his own car, and studying Business. Ruby is seventeen and will graduate high school this year. Kyle is fifteen and dying to drive like his brother. Dawn is thirteen and aspires to be an exchange student. Our kind and compassionate youngest child. If she goes, I'll miss her terribly.

It's becoming increasingly real that my children's futures don't include me. I may have created them with my body, but I don't own them, and never did. Mothers through the ages have had to let their babies go. Yet every emerging generation will experience anew the same sharp edge of separation. And so, the world turns.

Erika offers to make coffee. She fills an electric kettle and, using a small grinder which she fills with fresh beans, she makes a loud buzz for thirty seconds.

'What happened to your hand grinder? And the rocket stove to boil the kettle?'

I recall the day Erika put her Mrs Potts iron on the wood stove to press some shirts.

'We're selective. A few new toys have come along,' says Erika with a shrug, 'but we keep in practice. The old tools are still on the shelf.'

We talk about all the people who were part of the movement, and where they are now. Jenny Gamble is Professor of Midwifery at Griffith University, preparing to take long service leave. Jocelyn Toohill left the Mater to run the Gold Coast Birth Centre and is now Director of Midwifery for Queensland Health. FBC member, Melissa Fox, established Health Consumers Queensland amplifying consumer partnership with health services for better outcomes. Their advocacy helped women with pelvic mesh complications via the first co-designed multidisciplinary clinic in Australia, funded by the Queensland Government. She advocated for legal abortion in Queensland, and the Termination of Pregnancy Act was adopted in December 2018. She also advocates for the Queensland Council for LGBTI Health. Her long-time colleague, Jo Smethurst, is the Senior Engagement Advisor at HCQ.

Liz Wilkes from Toowoomba founded MyMidwives, the largest network of midwives in Australia, providing pregnancy, birth and postnatal care under the provisions of Medicare. She still lobbies for suitable indemnity insurance.

Dr Sarah Buckley travels the globe as an author doing speaking tours on hormones and ecstasy in childbirth.

Founding midwife at the Birth Centre, Marg Fien, retired several years ago, aged 74, unable to count the number of babies she caught in her 35-year career. Her colleague Karen Marshall is preparing to retire in 2020. Some of the midwives I met via Maternity Coalition now work in remote Indigenous communities, or volunteer in maternity clinics in Africa.

Tamara has returned to her calling at the Birth Centre.

'What about you, Erika? You're a midwife at the Royal now, what's it like?'

'Sometimes I'm a fish out of water but I love my work. I'm supporting mothers to create happy, healthy families.'

In 2018, with continuous pestering by the consumer groups, the Royal installed the new, deep, state of the art birth pools in the birth suites: fourteen years after the waterbirth protest, seventeen years since the supposed error was discovered in the first place. At least we can proudly point out, 'See that deep, oval bath in your room? You're entitled to use it.' Well, if your midwife on shift is credentialed for it. Bureaucracy, not safety, still limits access to the new tubs in the birth suite at the Royal, for consumers and midwives.

After the Roxon reforms, Maternity Coalition lost focus as an organisation and disbanded in an avalanche of petty internal politics, splitting into separate organisations: Maternity Choices Australia and Maternity Consumer Network, for years representing different agendas. Consumer advocate, Alicia Staines, convenes the Maternity Consumer Network, the new peak consumer body representing birth in Australia.

Despite policy support for midwifery, the old obstetric culture continues to block autonomy of practice. A prominent Australian obstetrician recently referred to midwifery as 'witchcraft' – denying evidence of benefit from the use of complementary medicine like acupuncture. 'The Killing Fields' continues to nip at our heels.

Coffee and biscuits become lunch as we reminisce about what might have been for women and midwives, and what could possibly still come to pass. Access to midwifery care in Australia has increased from 1% to 8% in 20 years. In Queensland, 20% of women use midwifery models of care, provided by 16% of the midwifery workforce. Progress is incremental but moving in the right direction.

In future health, hospital beds will be prioritised to the sick while midwives conduct house calls and run clinics for their local health districts. Or midwives could operate free-standing birth centres, maintaining respectful, collaborative relationships with their district hospitals. They'll one day attend women where they live, with the authority to support women to stay home to birth. And first nation's people will have cultural practices integrated and respected in the continuum of their maternity care.

In an age of global uncertainty, empowering mothers will protect our future. Our children won't be passengers when they have their own children. They'll be able to access a broad range of information that gives them the greatest sense of confidence and safety and be supported in their choices.

When I notice the glow on the horizon, I take my leave. Driving home, I wonder how many midwives and advocates from that time would enjoy a reunion and an opportunity to tell their version of this story.

Dear reader, you hold my heart in your hands. This is my story, but it isn't about me at all.

In telling just one version of this story there are, of course, many other events that contributed to the movement and people whose omission is only because, at the time, we didn't directly work together. I'd like to thank the individuals who permitted their true names and stories to be attached to a characterisation in this retelling. I hope I have validated your quiet achievements.

Thank you to the people whose names were changed or omitted for the sake of simplicity, anonymity, or a streamlined experience for readers.

Thank you to all the past and present members of Friends of the Birth Centre Assoc, allies in the Home Midwifery Association, The Australian College of Midwives, Maternity Coalition, plus all our partners and children whose stories are real and true, even though names have been changed. My sincere apologies to Dr. David Molloy, Janet Fraser, Kath Bannan, 'Tamara', 'Claudia', and 'Olivia' for reconstructing your grief. I struggled with the decision to include your stories and I know you all struggled with being included. It could have been any of us in different circumstances.

This book took ten years to write and wouldn't have been finished without the inspirational support of Mary-Lou Stephens and cunning editing by Sue Goldstiver.

Thank you to my beta readers, sensitivity readers, editors and fact-checkers: Margie Riley, Lauren E Daniels, Elizabeth Barnett, Ashley Gill, Megan Warren, Ruth Morgan, Tessa Bobir, Cathoel Jours, Leisl Leighton,
Dom Balwin, Lisa Morgan, and Samantha Elley.

Thank you to my husband Paul and our beautiful family.

And to my beautiful mother, who bravely gave her consent to publish.
We live in the same town now and remain actively involved in each other's lives.

WHAT DOES IT FEEL LIKE BEING BORN?
A memoir of maternity activism

Shawline Publishing Group Pty Ltd
www.shawlinepublishing.com.au

CPSIA information can be obtained
at www.ICGtesting.com
Printed in the USA
LVHW031709111120
671416LV00010B/1736